CW01673520

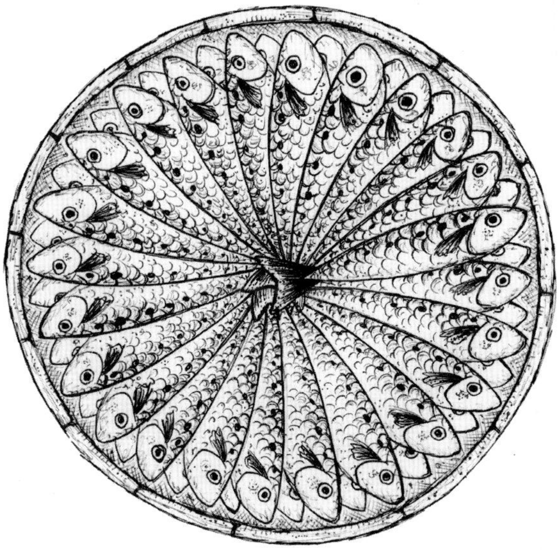

SALTY COVE

MEVAGISSEY

Mevagissey Bay (Porthiley, 1694)

Porth Hyly, 'saltwater cove'

Images Matt Facey and Sally Mitchell

Words Barbara Hocking, Jill Edwards, Julian Waring and Mark Sweeney

Inspiration Lauren Hunkin

Everyone involved in the making of this book did so voluntarily. The volunteers loaned their skill and time to enable all proceeds to the charity, the Fishermen's Mission. On behalf of the charity, our sincere and heartfelt thanks to the volunteers who created the content and style of this book. Their consciousness and determination are in the ink that runs through every page. They strove tirelessly to give back to Mevagissey something that everyone should be proud of and to raise important donations to the Fishermen's Mission.

We'd like to thank all those who supported the publication costs of the book through the crowdfunding effort at the start of 2022.

www.fishermensmission.org.uk

The history books say that Mevagissey was born and raised on fishing. The founding and growth of the village has always centred around fishermen and the sea. It is not surprising that the word so strongly associated with Mevagissey is 'pilchard'. This one catch was an industry in itself, with the oily fish being much sought after by the Europeans and its oil being used to fuel the streetlamps of London.

Against this backdrop it is hardly surprising that we find fishing is still part of the deep and rich heritage of this beautiful part of Cornwall today. The fishermen and women of Mevagissey, active and now retired, their families and friends are still very much the backbone of this wonderful village.

This book is our third of its kind, following on from 'Salt of the Earth' (Newlyn) and 'Sea, Salt and Solitude' (North East Cornwall) respectively. Each is very different as you would expect, a reflection of the differences in the communities and their histories.

Salty Cove is equally as beautiful, full of rich imagery and wonderful memories – both of the past and the present. Publications such as these are, however, born from the hard work and commitment (mostly voluntary) of many hands and minds.

The very talented photographers, Matt Facey and Sally Mitchell have given many, many hours of their time to perfect the images in the book, giving a rare visual insight into what really makes up a community in a small Cornwall fishing village. Lauren Hunkin, Barbara Hocking and Jill Edwards have together faithfully scripted the words of those you see in the photographs, so the story truly flows.

Much as he would prefer me not mention him, I must again pay tribute to our Regional Fundraising Manager for Cornwall and Devon, Julian Waring, whose heart and soul remains interwoven in the pages. Another 'Mission Man' who will be long remembered.

I know you will enjoy this book as much as I have, and to each and every single person who has contributed in any and every way: a heartfelt thank you.

The Fishermen's Mission is a very special charity and we couldn't do our work without you.

ALI GODFREY

DIRECTOR OF BUSINESS DEVELOPMENT
FISHERMEN'S MISSION

FOREWORD

In 1951, the Festival of Britain year, the Mevagissey Octet was asked to sing at Caxton Hall in London to represent fishermen at a service for the Mission of Deep Sea Fishermen. The eight men were Jim Hunkin, Ambrose Pollard, Dick Hunkin, Norman Rowe, Joe Roberts, Martin Chesterfield, Percy Mitchell and Tom Crowle: all Mevagissey men, and all delighted to accept the offer.

Just two or three years beforehand, Dick's brother John Francis Hunkin was lost at sea and local fishermen acknowledged the good work of the Fishermen's Mission in looking after his family. Some five years later, Dick himself was lost at sea with both men listed on the role of honour at the mission in Newlyn.

Any organisation which helps fishermen to keep safe deserves our assistance, and so I had no hesitation in accepting the request to write this Foreword. In the words of my dad, Ambrose, when he worked out of Newlyn, "You could always rely on the chat and a cup of tea at the mission."
RIP Ginge.

GEOFF POLLARD

RAGLAVAR

Yn 1951, an vledhen may feu synsys Gool Bretan ynni, gelwys veu an Mevagissey Octet dhe gana yn Hel Caxton yn Loundres, avel kannasow pyskadoryon yn servis a-barth an Ganaseth a Byskadoryon Mor Down. An eth den na o Jim Hunkin, Ambrose Pollard, Dick Hunkin, Norman Rowe, Joe Roberts, Martin Chesterfield, Percy Mitchell ha Tom Crowle. Tus a Lannvorek ens i oll, ha fest lowen dhe assentya dhe'n galow.

Saw ogas ha diw po teyr bledhen kynsa y feu kellys y'n mor broder Dick, John Francis Hunkin y hanow, ha'n byskadoryon leel a aswonas gras a ober da Kanaseth an Varners neb re vagsa y deylu. Nebes pymp bledhen a-wosa y feu kellys y'n mor Dick y honan ha skrifys yw henwyn an dhew war rol an dus a vri y'n Ganaseth yn Lulynn.

Y tegoodh dhyn ni porres gweres an kowethyansow oll a hwil gwitha an byskadoryon, ytho ny wrug vy hockya vyth dge assentya dhe skrifa an raglavar ma. Dell leveri ow thas vy, Ambrose y hanow, hag ev owth oberi a-dhyworth Lulynn y honan, "pupprys y hyllys fydhya war geskows ha hanafas a de y'n Ganaseth."

Re gosko 'Ginge' yn kres.

GEOFF POLLARD

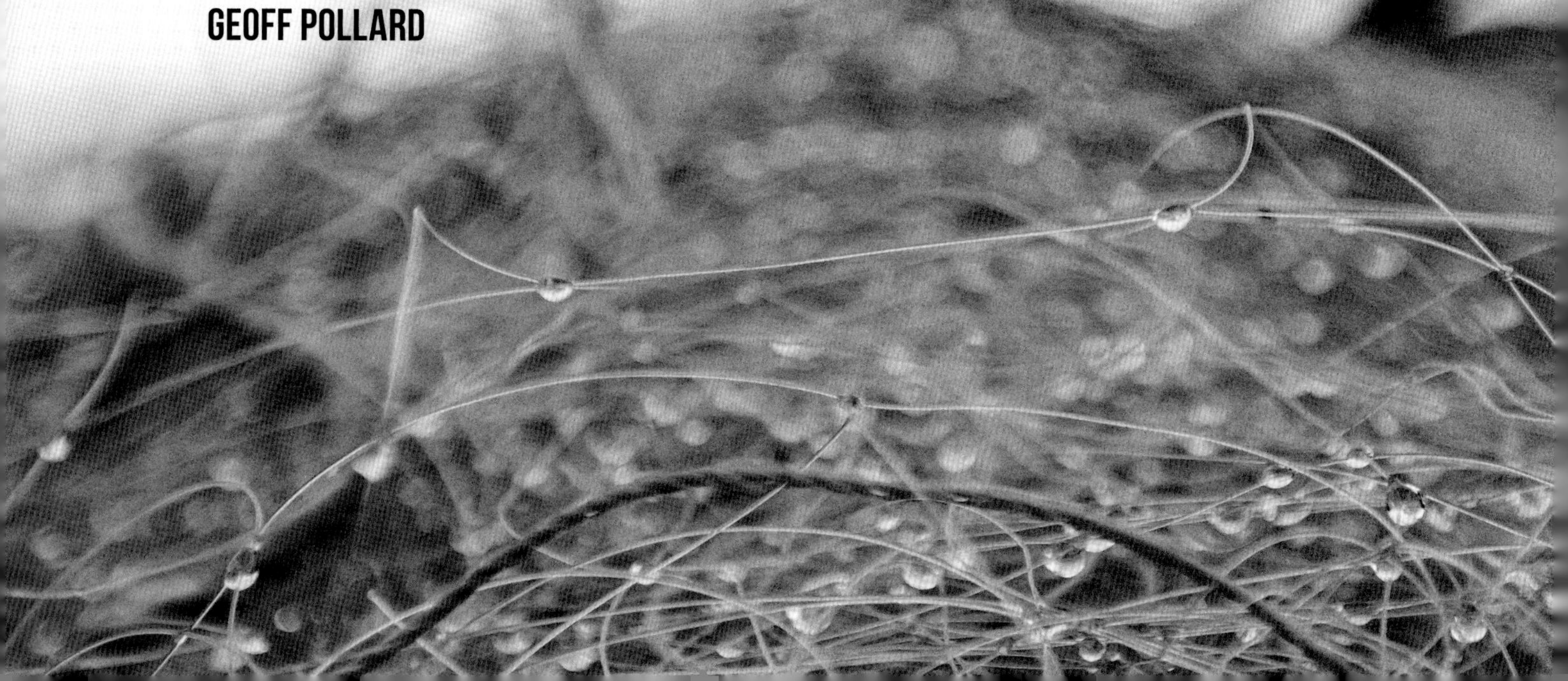

INTRODUCTION

Wandering through my new hometown of Porthleven in 2011, I heard the noises of a launch party in a gallery for the book 'Harbour 2 Harbour', by David and Janet Penprase. This was their second fundraising book of portraits featuring the people of Porthleven. I was impressed by the strong black and white images of the local residents combined with their interesting life stories. Walking my dog through the town I would see a poster of the book with updated sales figures, and soon thousands of pounds of sales became tens of thousands. It was incredible that this book and its predecessor 'Harbour to Harbour' has raised such valued donations, of around £60,000, for Cornish hospices.

I started working for the Fishermen's Mission in 2011 and based in Newlyn, I was glad to be not only managing the Centre in Newlyn but also enacting the work of the charity and its fundraising. Three years later, the strong memory of the two Porthleven books was still in my mind, so I approached David and Jan and invited them over to the Centre with the thought of asking if they would consider volunteering their time and expertise to a third book, based in Newlyn.

It was fascinating to hear about how the Porthleven books started, that their retirement project, utilising David's skills as a photographer, was to record 100 portraits (of Porthleven town folk) but ended up capturing around 1100 faces. David and Jan had worked collaboratively within their community not only to raise the funds to print the books but also to realise their vision to other volunteers. Prior to printing, many hours were spent poring over its design and layout; individuals or groups were interviewed; and their stories proofread by volunteers and finally collated by Rita Collier. It was obvious that their previous business experience, hard work and drive were such that it created a piece of social history, a local archive along with the charities receiving substantial donations. The books are a wonderful representation and gift to the townspeople of Porthleven.

Well from that first meeting I could tell they were really interested in the fishing community, and within six months 'Salt of the Earth' was launched to a very busy opening party in the November of 2014. The book had to be reprinted in six weeks and the overall donation was just under £40,000.

It's testimony to David and Jan's hard work and vision that there's a continuation of their original book format. The word 'Salt' has continued, from the Newlyn book 'Salt of the Earth', to the North Cornish book 'Sea Salt and Solitude' by volunteer photographer Chris Hewitt and volunteer writer Deborah Richards, and now to this collaborative book in Mevagissey, 'Salty Cove'.

Our thanks to David & Jan, on behalf of the charity, for loaning the concept of their books and passing on their experiences to benefit The Fishermen's Mission in terms of considerable donations, and also for the bringing together of each community to celebrate their culture and their achievements in a clever and beautiful art form.

JULIAN WARING

FUNDRAISING MANAGER FOR CORNWALL, FISHERMEN'S MISSION

This book is dedicated to the men who gave their lives,
who paid the true price of the fish on your plate.

Let us not forget their families who are left behind.

RODNEY INGRAM

FISHERMAN

"I started fishing when I was six years old, when I could swim from the slipway to the rocks and back again"

That was when I could catch crabs and hang around with the other lads around the harbour. At the age of ten, I had a little punt with outboard motor and went fishing for pollock. At twelve I worked on the *Christabel* fishing every night through the summer holidays in the evenings; I used to scoop up all the pilchards that fell out of the nets. When I was fourteen, another lad hurt his back and I was taken on a half share, as a crew member. You'd have four people on the boat, after all the expenses, gear and costs; you would share the catch equally and fairly. After my first week I took home £15. My dad was a craftsman for the local council who earned £6. 10s. 0d. a week old money.

I went to grammar school and then onto Naval College in Plymouth and went away to sea as a Communications Officer at 19 years old for ten years; but got married and came home to Mevagissey and got a boat from John Moor in 1972 until I had my family. I then worked in electronics with British Telecom for 25 years and got a pension, and got a 22-foot boat since retiring. I go out when I want catching pollock from December to May and bass from May onwards.

I have been a Mevagissey Harbour Trustee for the past ten years.

ALEX INGRAM
FISHERMAN

"I didn't have much choice getting into fishing growing up. My dad was a fisherman, and my uncle Rodney, and my grandfather his side. The book called 'Whistle the Wind' by Ken Shearwood: the main character was my great-grandad 'George Alan', my Nan's granddad. So I couldn't be anything else really"

Fishing is in my blood, and if Dad was on a boat, I was too. He only had a small open boat, unless he was working for Dave Hunkin commercially and when he was younger still, for Chris Chesterfield. But as I got older and we worked together, we didn't get on so well; 'a conflict of interest', but we were always together. I was 18 years old when I went full time fishing.

I work on Matt Hunkin's boat now but initially ran the boat for him called the *Leonora* and then the *Darter*, a larger boat for a couple years. Then Matt bought the *Provider* and I ran it for a couple years before he left working for his dad and we have worked together for the past couple of years, with Matt as the skipper. It works really well 'most of the time' and it's easier for me with Matt making the decisions.

I wouldn't want to do anything else now. I have gotten so used to doing fishing, I don't have to think about it. You can change your mind when it's blowing a gale and lashing with rain, but day to day I enjoy it. I normally look forward to it. I hope my child grows up the same way as all us young fishermen now together, as good friends, enjoying happy times. We shall see.

FRAN INGRAM

DOG GROOMER & FISHERMAN'S WIFE

"Life married to a fisherman is definitely an interesting one and certainly isn't for everyone. One thing I have definitely learnt is that when they say they are going for a lunch time pint, don't expect them home for tea!"

Alex works with the tides, so I know when I'm going to have peace and quiet for a week and I don't have to listen to the snoring. It makes a difference knowing when he's going be away or not; it does make life a little easier as you can make plans, etc! Even when he is home, he will quite often be doing jobs down the quay; well so he says, but quite often you know the day will start with a coffee and chat in the Harbour Tavern or stood on the jetty around someone's truck chatting!

Since being together with Alex, I have gained some of the best friends with the other fishermen's partners and it's now exciting to see their children, the next generation, all growing up together, just like our generation did.

With Alex often being away at sea, parenting can sometimes be a bit of a struggle, but seeing the smile on our little boy's face when Alex returns, I know it's all worth it.

JAMIE 'TABBY' TABB

FORMER FISHERMAN & SKIPPER

"Me and Alex Ingram had a little punt we worked together; we'd be putting out baskets for prawns behind East Quay. We all grew up together, went to school together and fished together"

I had gone to college and gained my qualifications as a gamekeeper and groundsman; but went straight into fishing, handlining on Alex Ingram's boat the *Irene*. Then I'd done pilcharding with Matt Hunkin and usually got seasick on his boat the *Pimpernel*! I then worked for John Williams on his boat for a couple years and then worked for James Saunders on the *Red Vixen*. One experience I remember was when we had to be rescued by the RNLI miles off the Lizard. We were taking on water into the front compartment where the bunk beds were to. All our mattresses and pillows were floating around. We were lucky it was daylight because it was scary enough; we were bailing out the water as fast as it was coming in but luckily it didn't touch the engine and kept the pumps that were working, going! We took on 3000 litres of sea water! The RNLI rescued us and pumped us out and were so relieved and will always be thankful and grateful to the RNLI.

Then I was able to buy my own boat the *Jade Star* and skippered her for about six years and just sold her, because I have changed tack in careers and now running a countryside servicing business and retained fireman and really busy!

MARCUS WIXEY JNR

FISHERMAN

The skipper of *Venture*. I grew up in a house on the waterfront in a small village in Plymouth called Turnchapel. A memory I have is of my dad pushing me out in a punt at around the age of four and watching as I taught myself how to row and I suppose that's where it all started! From then on the boats grew one step at a time until I started going to sea with my dad while still at school, living on the Isle of Wight at the time.

I feel from a small boat working your way up is how all good fishermen develop; you just can't beat the knowledge you gain from being exposed to the wind and the tide and completely at one with the elements. While writing this I'm sat at the wheel of my family's stern trawler while towing our net 20 miles south of Plymouth at the age of 26. Who knows what the future of the fishing industry holds? – but personally I am full of optimism.

MARCUS WIXEY SNR

FISHERMAN

I got into fishing by accident really. I always had boats and was a keen scuba diver. I had a small boat and was fishing as a sideline to pay for her upkeep. It soon became full-time. My wife, Sue, claims that I was at sea the afternoon of my son's birth; she exaggerates. It was, in fact, the following morning. Living on the waterfront in Turnchapel I thought it would be a good idea to fit out a new hull in the garden, while my son Marcus Jnr, a baby at the time, watched on from his play pen. I'm sure he learnt a lot from the experience – certainly some colourful language!

After owning many other boats and fishing from many harbours my son and I now own the trawler *Venture*, but he runs her. There can only be one skipper.

ALAN FURSE

FISHERMAN

"Fishing... I'm glad I did what I did, I would have done the same again"

Alan has lived his whole life in Mevagissey. He was born next door to where he now lives in a cottage on The Cliff. Although Alan was keen to become a fisherman, his parents wanted him to learn a trade, so he began an apprenticeship in boat-building at Percy Mitchell's boatyard in Portmellon.

After completing his apprenticeship as a shipwright at 20 years old, he spent nine months in his spare time in the evenings and at weekends building his own fishing boat which he named *Superb*. It was a 22-foot open fishing boat with a 7ft 8in beam, powered by a diesel engine. The planking was made of mahogany and it had brass fittings.

"At 21 I became a full-time fisherman and ten years later in 1976, I built my next fishing boat which became *Superb 2*, which is the one I still use for fishing today. I have always been mad about boats. I like drawing and painting them as a hobby."

Some of Alan's painting skills adorn the cottage walls, pictures of boats – personal favourites – painted on slate. He is very modest about his talent!

"I go fishing throughout the year, sometimes early in the morning or in the evening, sometimes with another crew member. I fish for mackerel, squid and bass and a few others. In the summer high season I run boat trips around the bay for the tourists. Fishing is unpredictable. If you have a good week one week you got to look after it, you might not go out the next week, you need to work your money."

SHARMAN FURSE

FISHERMAN'S WIFE

"The funfair was an important part of my family's history"

Sharman was a Newquay girl. "My parents ran a B&B in the town at a time when they offered an evening meal to residents plus lunch on a Sunday. I remember as a little girl my husband, Alan, coming over with his father, a fish hawker from Mevagissey, selling fish to my mother which was used in the preparation of meals."

Sharman is proud of her heritage. It was her maternal grandfather, Joe Rowland, who started up

the funfair under the name of J.Rowland and Son which was based in St Austell and today is one of the oldest in the West Country. Her cousin still runs part of the business. "Many years ago the steam engines could be seen out on Lighthouse Quay during Feast Week and in more recent times the funfair would come down to the festival and set up on what is now the football field."

Sharman recognises how fishing has changed in Mevagissey; where boys would follow their fathers into fishing, the fishing industry has become more challenging with prices of fish fluctuating and restrictions with rules and regulations. However, she is pleased that recently there are more younger men joining the fishing fleet.

"It is a very different life being married to a fisherman and like many, Alan lives and breathes fishing. We may be having an in-depth conversation about a topic but no matter what it is, he will turn it around to fishing or fishing boats!

When he has been out mackerel fishing and he comes home, he absolutely stinks! But I still love him."

MIKE ROBERTS

MEVAGISSEY BOY

"I can't help it somehow, getting involved; it must be something in me!"

Since my teens I have been involved with community events. I've always had a sense of duty towards Mevagissey: youngest committee member of the Social Club and treasurer for many years. I helped create a playing field from the village dump and, in the 50s, with the start of the Feast Week as we know it today. My great love was swimming and water polo. From my national service in the RAF, working life then started in the china clay industry, eventually retiring as the Marketing Systems Manager. Together with my wife, I ran the Haven Restaurant and Guest House in Fore Street during the 60s and 70s. I also qualified as a swimming teacher and subsequently became head coach of St Austell swimming club. I was one of the founder members of the Mevagissey Rowing Club and later Chairman. In 1972 I was elected Restormel district councillor and served for 15 years. During this period, Mevagissey Parish Council was re-formed, and I am now its Chairman, together with Chairman of The Jubilee Hall and a member of the Harbour Board of Trustees.

Mevagissey is a very special place. I have always worked to preserve its special character, while accepting that some changes are inevitable.

VICTORIA O'SHEA & KIRSTY WAKEHAM

MEVAGISSEY FEAST WEEK COMMITTEE

"'See you Feast Week?' is a question asked between family and friends of Mevagissey. Feast Week is for the village, not for tourists or businesses, the community!"

Mevagissey has celebrated the feast of St Peter since 1754. It has evolved into a wonderful community event, where we welcome locals, exiles and visitors to join us in the celebrations. Originally this was purely a religious festival, where every denomination would have a 'Feast Day' with children's sports and feast tea. We had five churches or chapels, and it took up the whole week but it gradually died away with the demise of the chapels.

However, it's thanks to Francis Hunkin in the 70s, who formed a committee and revived it, and his son Robin, who continued it as chairman for creating the success it is today. Now, the Fish Feast Sunday itself features parades, exhibitions, demonstrations, live music and lots of fish dishes to eat. Other events through the week include teas, flora dances, choirs and bands, flower displays, children's entertainment, competitions, colourful carnival, trawler and raft races, a fête and a huge firework display.

The Feast Week Committee today is made up of 12 volunteers, including the chairman, secretary, treasurer and individuals responsible for each relevant aspect of the week's events, working closely with the village and army of wonderful volunteers needed to coordinate the events safely.

Kirsty and Victoria have worked on the committee for over 20 years and truly enjoy their involvement, from getting up on Feast Sunday at 5am, checking the weather and starting their involvement from 7am, until the following Saturday night, when the firework display ends the event. Both say they are full of emotion then that it's over, and another successful Feast Week concluded.

MIKE SHEPHERD

FOUNDER OF KNEEHIGH THEATRE

"I still think of Mevagissey as a strong place of community"

My parents moved to St Austell not long after the end of the Second World War, when I was one. My dad used to describe Mevagissey as the Wild West and we weren't allowed to go there as kids, so of course we desperately wanted to go! As teenagers we would cycle over to Meva and for me, it was always an exciting place to be with a strong community centred around the harbour. With Kneehigh Theatre, we started doing events for Mevagissey Feast Week. This would have been around 1980.

The first one we did, I played a spiv from London called Sid Power who had brought with him the world's most incredible stuntman. The stuntman was played by a young and very fit guy called John Mergler, who was involved in our early shows and events. There was a crowd on the jetty and Sid Power's stuntman came zapping down Polkirt Hill on a bicycle with this flare, given to us by Tony Arden the brilliant local coastguard at the time. He shot down Jetty Street and hit a ramp with the idea that he'd jump from the jetty over to East Quay, of course this was impossible. We had Barney Potter helping out, he had a black powder licence and used to blow things up. There was a massive explosion as the stuntman flew off the ramp prompting a spectacular pyrotechnic display and seagulls flapping wings and raucous cries as they wheeled around the harbour. There was smoke everywhere. I'd borrowed a punt from a fisherman and we'd anchored it in the middle of the harbour. As the smoke cleared it revealed the bottom half of a tailor's dummy, upside-down with feet in the air as if our stuntman had gone headfirst through the bottom of the punt! I'm not sure you'd be allowed to pull off stunts like this anymore.

I've always thought that Mevagissey was a place where you could make things happen... it was fun! I still think of Mevagissey as a strong place of community. I have a real attachment to it.

CAROLE HALLIDAY BEM

MEVAGISSEY YOUTH CLUB LEADER

"It's been lovely to watch the children grow up in the Youth Club and now see them bring their children. And what a pleasure it's been over the years. We've had some good laughs and most kids are such great fun"

1989 there was a group of us started a Mevagissey Youth Club in the Old Chapel, thinking it would just be open every third week to supervise badminton. From the moment we opened we've remained so every week since. When the chapel was converted into flats, we moved to the old school. Then when the school was converted into apartments, we moved into the Jubilee Hall and been there since and was much better for our needs.

Activities ranged across volleyball, netball, quizzes, hockey, football, table tennis, snooker and games we'd create for them. Parents would ask, "What age can the kids join?" My reply would be, "Age six until they can't behave themselves!"

In the past we have organised discos, swimming at a hotel at Carlyon Bay and even ice skating in Plymouth. My friend Ruby (60 years young) always wanted to try ice skating; she was doing really well, no hanging on the edges for Ruby. She went everywhere on the rink. After about 30 minutes (I remained clinging to the sides) she fell backwards, cut her head and blood spread so fast on the ice! Everyone had to leave the ice and a machine cleared up the blood! We went skiing twice at Plymouth – but no Ruby! Even took them to Alton Towers twice and invited other Youth Clubs in the area to join us and the children would pay in instalments for the trip. One year we took three coaches and a double-decker bus! We'd go on an overnight bus and never lost one child!

MEVAGISSEY PARISH COUNCIL

The Parish Councils were re-formed in the late 1970s, after being disbanded in the mid-1930s. The Parish Council has been in existence, in its current form, since then and Mike Roberts, the present Chairman, was partly responsible for its re-formation in the 70s. Mike was the District Councillor at this time and able to set the process in motion for re-forming Mevagissey Parish Council. Tom Dudley was the first Chairman of the Parish Council in its present form.

The Parish Council acts in the interest of all aspects of public life, within its limited resources and its professional powers, which of course are considerable within the budgetary constraints we have available; which means we can employ a clerk and pay towards certain needs of the Parish. Our largest undertaking in recent years is the public toilets. When Cornwall Council decided they weren't obliged to run them and gave the responsibility to others, we were forced to take them on through necessity. It's a fairly costly operation for a small community; hence the increased Mevagissey council tax.

We have been given greater responsibilities for planning and development matters and are very conscious of the way in which the village is developed; hence the 'Neighbourhood Plan' that the Parish Council produced and is proving to be very effective. This remains an important role of the Parish Council.

JAMES MUSTOE

CORNWALL COUNCILLOR FOR MEVAGISSEY AND ST AUSTELL BAY

"Mevagissey's identity has always been and always will be, about its fishing industry. It's the centre of the community and the heartbeat of the village"

James comes from Mevagissey and lived on Cliff Street. As a child he played in the harbour when the tide was out.

"As a councillor I am even more involved with the harbour shops, and very involved with the life of the harbour and its community, involving others with harbour clean-ups.

The harbour is the centre of the fishing and not just a tourist attraction. It's a living, breathing community hub. The inner and outer harbours are both very special and something that we don't see anywhere else around the south coast of Cornwall. It's also the people who make it so special; they work around the harbour and it's important we have such a young fishing community: it's unique. Cornish fishing life makes Mevagissey stand out. Young men I went to school with are now fishing: it's their livelihood. It passes from generation to generation. You see families like the Chesterfields handing it down and that is amazing.

I am married to a lovely Cornish woman, Laura Mustoe, whose father was the Harbour Master for thirty years or more and is now on the Harbour Trust. I just love Mevagissey and the whole area that surrounds it. In my spare time I love to walk around the place. Today I have walked from Pentewan to Mevagissey and up to Heligan, and then this interview, before going to a Parish meeting. I get a great deal of satisfaction being the Mevagissey Councillor."

HUGH ST AUBYN BOWLES

MEVAGISSEY HARBOUR MASTER 1992 -2013

"Mevagissey harbour is one of the finest in the world. I've sailed worldwide in my career, I think I am in a position to assess that"

Hugh has lived in Cornwall all of his life. Following his O levels, he joined Trident Tankers as an apprentice navigating cadet and for all his deep-sea career stayed with the P&O group. During part of his career, after promotion through the ranks, he managed 12 Abu Dhabi tankers. In 1977 he was promoted to Chief Officer and six years later given the title of Captain. Sadly, his time at sea was to be cut short due to the death of his first wife and Hugh came ashore to look after their four children. "I turned my carpentry hobby into a business and started to make bespoke furniture and kitchens for people in the local area using my basement as a workshop." Unfortunately, after six years the 80s recession hit and this was no longer viable.

After working for a short time in Falmouth, in 1992 Hugh took on the job as Mevagissey Harbour Master, a post which he retained for 22 years until December 2013. During this time, he met Sue and his family grew from four to six children! "Mevagissey Harbour was a lovely place to work. It was a challenging job but during my time as Harbour Master we made lots of improvements assisted by grant aid. These included in 1998 extending the building of the seaward side of Lighthouse Quay, building the net lofts, modernising the chill and cold store and extending the jetty."

In 2004 the aquarium, which had been rebuilt using a Lottery Heritage Grant, was opened by the Mayor of London. "We decided we should have a film of the fishing industry showing in the background. We gained archive footage from TSW (Television South West) of the pilchard fishing. Chris in the harbour office produced a video of Ocean Fish in Roche to show the modern-day fishing industry, and from BBC Spotlight we requested some filming of the *Resolute* catching pilchards with ring nets which they had filmed for television. When it was all put together, I did the voice over. I was to discover the only way to do this in a quiet place, away from chatter and phones in the Harbour Office, was on the toilet!" So, when you visit the aquarium bear this in mind!

"I have the greatest respect for all fishermen. Wild horses wouldn't drag me to sea. They do a tremendous job and especially in poor weather, they are risking their lives. They earn every penny they make."

CHRIS GILBERTSON

CLERK TO THE HARBOUR TRUSTEES

Chris's main task is to maintain everyday paperwork and administration of the harbour, which includes wages, bills, invoices and letters all involving the harbour's business. He believes the fishing industry is a very important part of the harbour, explaining how the income of the harbour is split four ways with fishing revenue, moorings revenue, parking revenue and Aquarium donations.

The harbour has existed since 1774, formed as a 'Harbour Trust' in the Ship Inn, and the original leather-bound ledgers still exist in the office. The harbour has changed a lot, but remains original at the same time, and is at full capacity; they couldn't rent another inch of the harbour. Chris explains that the facility was originally a 'Fishing Beach' prior to being a harbour. The inner walls meant it was protected and in the mid-1800s, the outer pool harbour walls were built to protect it from the south-easterly winds. At this time there was even a photographic studio on the outer, which sold photos for postcards, so the harbour's history was recorded photographically. In particular the boats prior to engines, such as the luggers, were so packed in together it was said you could walk across their decks from one side of the harbour to the other.

The 'pool', as the outer harbour is termed, at low tide is 2.3 metres deep and has stayed the same within an inch over the past one hundred years. It never needs dredging. After storm Emma in 2018 all the sand disappeared and exposed the rock bed, but it has gradually returned on the tide.

The success of the fishing fleet is the adaptability of the boats. They are able to change their method of fishing overnight, where other fleets aren't able to. In Newlyn you have beam trawlers and they only fish that way. Mevagissey boats can switch between beam, cod or bass gear, or use lines or pots. That is why fishing in Mevagissey is so successful, with an increasing fleet and more young people coming into the industry, compared with other places where the young are moving away.

"There is a lot of work that goes into ensuring the safety of fishing crews and the public, with a constant juggling act to keep the harbour tidy, efficient, working and safe"

SIMON ELLIOT

ASSISTANT HARBOUR MASTER

"This is my dream job, always has been"

I grew up in Sheffield where I lived for the first 50 years of my life. I ran my own company, recycling plastic. Since I was four years old, my family holidayed in Mevagissey or Portmellon, often visiting four or five weeks of the year and so I made many friends down here. Five years ago, I decided to move down here permanently, firstly taking on the role as Pier Master in Falmouth with the council and then after various other jobs, I applied for and got the job as Assistant Harbour Master in Mevagissey. Everyone on the harbour is so friendly; it is varied work and I really enjoy it. It's my dream job and always has been.

NEIL PROWSE

ASSISTANT HARBOUR MASTER

"I've done the same jobs as most of these fishing men, so I have a good understanding of the fishing industry and that makes my job on the harbour easier"

Mevagissey stands out as a strong and tight-knit community. I've lived in Mevagissey for 14 years, and until working with the harbour team, I hadn't appreciated just how close a community Mevagissey was, within the fishing fleet and their families. Mevagissey is primarily a Cornish fishing port, and that makes it unique these days. It's the second most productive fishing port in Cornwall, with about 60 fishing boats.

The harbour being a trust, and a charity, it depends greatly on the tourism, but primarily the income is from the fishermen. I appreciate that the harbour is a picturesque Cornish fishing port that remains relatively untouched, and the aim of the harbour staff is to maintain its originality, with unprotected walkways around the harbour, while maintaining its heritage and appearance.

I grew up in West Cornwall and as a boy, was connected closely with fishing and worked for a while on a Newlyn netter. I joined the Royal Navy from the age of 16 years old and saw the world, with a career spanning over ten years, before joining the Lighthouse Service for 24 years. My working life has always been connected with the sea, and I have gained extensive experience.

ANDREW TREVARTON

HARBOUR MASTER

"I'd like to have a small boat again. I do miss being out on the sea"

"In 1974 I moved with my family to Mevagissey as my father needed a larger fishing vessel which would be too big for the small harbour in Portloe where we lived, so he had a 30-foot boat built in John Moore's yard.

I attended Mevagissey School and then went on to Penrice. I wasn't interested in academic pursuits so at 16, in 1983, I left school and my father helped me to get my first boat. In order to have more experience, I worked on a boat with Peter Dudley, an experienced fisherman, for a couple of winters before settling back with my father on the *Sharon Rose*. In 1985, I purchased a larger vessel, a 35-foot crabber named the *Catherine Rose*, which was the last boat to have been built in Mitchell's Boatyard. I went on to buy a larger boat *Galatea*, but after 38 years of fishing, I sold her and in April 2021 took on the role of Mevagissey Harbour Master.

The role of Harbour Master is very different from what I was used to doing. Reaching my mid 50s, I'd had enough of working 60 or 70 miles offshore in the summer months. Fishing takes a toll, not only on your physical health but also on the family. Fishermen devote everything to fishing and family comes second. It was time for a change.

Since taking on the role, I am enjoying the position and hopefully making a difference and taking on new challenges. I have my staff who support me working out on the harbour and Chris in the office, who with his wealth of experience has helped me and made my job easier and more efficient. It is one of the best offices in the county with its views over the sea and the harbour."

Reflecting on incidents which have happened since Andrew took on the role, one in particular sticks in his mind. "Despite the signs up for no cycling on the harbour, there was an elderly gentleman who was scooting along on his electric bike when he swerved to avoid a lady and slipped with his bike over the harbour wall, fortunately landing in a muddy puddle. The staff and I were quickly on the scene. The gentleman had lost consciousness for about 30 seconds and when he came round, he looked straight up at me and said, 'I wasn't cycling on the quay, honest!' CCTV showed otherwise, but the important thing was he was ok and the next day, he returned to the office to thank us for looking after him."

Although Andrew is enjoying his new life as Harbour Master, it is obvious that part of him misses being out on his boat. At some stage he wants to buy a small boat so he can go out again but this time, for pleasure.

MARIA TREVARTON

NURSE & HARBOUR MASTER'S WIFE

"Andrew likes to be on the water and not in it and I like to be in it and not on it! He is my rock and anchor in life"

I always found it fascinating listening to Andrew's tales of fishing: the experiences and hard work and how he grew up with fishing with his own father. We got into married life easily together; he'd always go into port and wash or shower and stick his smelly clothes into a bin bag for washing and come home never smelling of fishing. Or maybe I've not got a good sense of smell!

The negatives are you can't make plans or include them in the plans. When we had Elizabeth, I relied on mine and Andrew's mother for support. He'd sometimes come home unexpectedly because he'd caught a boulder and wrecked his nets. No two days were ever the same; he'd always be watching the direction of the wind. He always reassured me he would never put himself in any real danger and I had faith in that fact. He has a real passion for fishing; it's in his blood. He's not a religious man but he'd say that is where he felt closest to God, at sea. It's a hard physical job and the stamina they need is incredible. I always tell him that if there was a doctorate for fishing he would have it, he's so knowledgeable. I just knew when I needed to just listen to him; I'd not have any solutions, just be his sounding board.

JAMES TREVARTON

FISHERMAN

"I've lived in Mevagissey my whole life and once I left school I became the fith generation of fishermen in my family"

I enjoy fishing because it is still a pretty free way of life. Once you're aboard the boat and away from the chaos of modern life it's peaceful and when it's all going right it's not a bad way to make a living. When things are not going too well or you have a breakdown with the boat, it's the opposite, which can be very stressful and financially worrying as I found out this year after purchasing my own boat and going single-handed. But even with the extra pressure it has been worth it, so I can spend more time at home with my wife Kay and daughter Isla, who the boat is named after, the *Isla Mei* FH7.

Mevagissey is a great place to grow up and I hope my daughter and possible future children have the same experiences growing up here as I did.

KAY TREVARTON

NURSE & FISHERMAN'S WIFE

"One of my favourite quotes that I feel accurately reflects our relationship... 'Distance teaches us to appreciate the days that we are able to spend together and distance teaches us the definition of patience'. It is a reminder that every moment together is special, and every second together should be cherished"

I'm always proud to tell people my husband is a fisherman and forever grateful of what he does, not only to provide for our family but to provide the world with seafood. Our generation is very lucky in regard to technology they use today that tracks them using AIS and phone tracking apps; because of this, it's not often I worry about James, as he is really knowledgeable and level-headed when it comes to working on the boat.

I can see the harbour from our living room window and I can see the boat pull up alongside the quay to land the catch. I used to grab the dogs quickly and run down and meet him. Now we have a daughter it's a little different. But I do what I can to help and even helped land fish a few times, and I have had a few phone calls over the years to pick him and his dad up from Brixham!

James has a new boat and works on his own, now that his dad is the Mevagissey Harbour Master. James has decided he wants to spend more time at home, to have more time with Isla our daughter, and to watch her grow up.

PHIL TREVARTON

"I didn't make a career of fishing, but had a big involvement in the family fishing trade. If you lived under father's roof, you had to help out"

"At eight years old, I would help in the evenings, making hand-made nets in the family lounge. We'd use the door handle, and a wooden board, and twine around the board; making a diamond shape mesh. When the net was 20 diamonds deep, you'd start again, working across the board, casting off when 30 foot in length.

Grandfather was a Portloe fisherman and the pilchard fishing was ending and he convinced my father to seek employment in a trade. So father took a 'shore' job, but he never forgot his dream of becoming a full-time fisherman.

Grandfather made his own withy pots, but father started with hand-made wooden pots called 'French barrels'. He soon found out that buying galvanised pots gave him more time at sea. You'd need over 300 pots to make a living in those days." Phil remembers as a young man, he finished a night shift and then drove off in a lorry to Totnes, to collect 330 partially finished pots and help make them up.

"Father with his knowledge of the fishing grounds, his summer work was potting for crab and lobster, and trammel net fishing; winter work was mackerel fishing. He would fish in the evenings off Portloe and was part of a beach seining crew, working the beaches between Porthscatho and Par."

CELIA MITCHELL

CHAIRPERSON OF THE HARBOUR TRUSTEES

"It's a wonderful community, a good local community all year round"

I grew up in a fishing family, spending my youth around the harbour and going on the boats. The harbour has been a big part of my life and all my family are, or were, fishermen. When I was 33, I joined the Cornwall Sea Fisheries as a representative of the MMO (Marine Management Organisation). After I'd been there a while, it so happened that the Harbour Trustees were looking for a representative of the Sea Fisheries and asked if I would join them to which I agreed. That was 13 years ago!

The trustees help maintain the harbour and are supportive of the fishermen. The harbour is the most important part of Mevagissey and keeping it a traditional working harbour, maintaining the sea walls and looking into new funding streams, is an important role of the trustees. It is the second biggest working fishing harbour in Cornwall. In fact in the 1900s it was the biggest!

The Harbour Trustees is a charity and because of this we can keep raising funds and keep it maintained for the village instead of it being put in the hands of a private enterprise. We are fortunate to have our own fishing facilities which is important for the fishermen.

Many of our fishermen come from fishing families and have been here for generations. We are fortunate that we have quite a number of younger people following their fathers into the industry here in Mevagissey.

CELIA MITCHELL

SELF-DRIVE BOATS

"Self-drive boats in Meva since 1947"

William Chesterfield started running the self-drive boats from the end of West Quay, now the fish quay, in about 1947. They eventually moved to the Aquarium slipway. There have been many different operators over the years. I started about 42 years ago with David Chesterfield and Jack Arthur. We had old wooden boats; all we had were life rings and a simple pump aboard. We eventually changed to fibreglass boats and at one time ran 22 boats. Nowadays, we have lifejackets and a rescue boat plus the use of mobile phones.

In the 1960s we would run from Whitsun up until October but now we just run in the summer holidays when families visit Mevagissey. We are restricted by the weather and conditions on the sea.

Many years ago, we had a 13-foot boat which we hired out to a couple. In those days we didn't take a deposit. After two hours, when they hadn't returned, we began to get worried so we took a search party out. I could see in the distance a boat out at sea and it was ours! On board was a lad of about nine years old and we brought him back to shore. It appears that the couple had taken the boat up onto the shore at Porthpean and left it. Some older teenagers had told the boy it was from Mevagissey and he should take it back. They started up the engine, pushed him off the beach and pointed in the direction of Mevagissey!

Thankfully, we have had no real dramas or accidents and running the boats over the years has been fun.

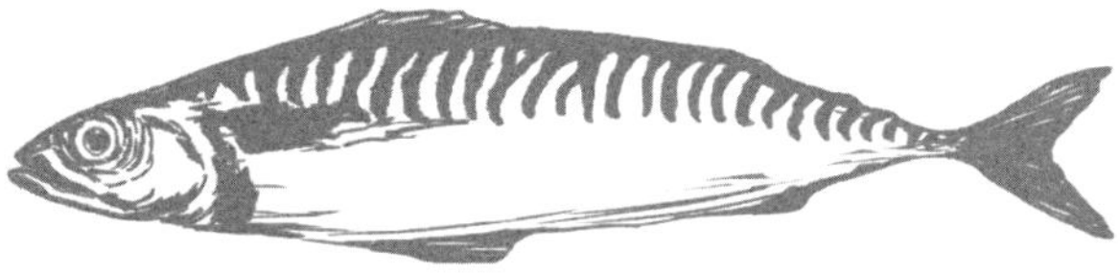

EDWARD MITCHELL

"I was in the Indian Ocean on a 300-metre container ship, 65-foot rolling waves crashing over the containers on the ship and heeling at a 25-degree angle, yeah I've experienced some harsh seas"

Fishing has always been in my family on both sides. Dad had the *Tamarisk* until 1996. It was a 12-metre trawling and scalloping boat. Mother had the self-hire boats, based near the slip by the Museum, for 35 years. I'd been out in a punt and boats from the age of 12 and wanted to go fishing but Dad said I needed to get some qualifications first.

I left Plymouth University with a BSc in Nautical Studies and gained my Unlimited Officer of the Watch which provides the required knowledge, skills and experience for seagoing employment as a Watchkeeping Officer in the Merchant Navy. My first job after university was in the Merchant Navy for five years and I've been working in the offshore industry for the last 17 years. I'm a Captain of a hydrographic survey vessel, 42 metres, with 18 personnel on board. I live in Mevagissey and work eight weeks on and eight weeks off, anywhere in Northern Europe. Working altogether like we do, you need a good sense of humour and an understanding of people. We can be fallible and stressed so I aim to be tolerant but maintain discipline, nipping little arguments in the bud before they get out of hand.

My wife Samantha has a skipper's licence. We've bought a Treeve 20-foot working boat called *Zara*. She's undergone a refurb and we're hoping to get out together, catch a bit of mackerel.

CHRIS HAMBLETT

RETIRED VET

"Mevagissey is a village that changes, it's a village with life in it"

When I met my partner Lorna, we both realised we had a love for Cornwall, and would visit for at least six weeks of the year, alternating between Veryan and Mevagissey. On a lone visit to Mevagissey in 2004, I saw my house on The Cliff for sale. I put in an offer which was accepted and then returned to Wiltshire to give Lorna the good news! I left my vet's practice in Devizes and we moved down in January 2005. We were very happy until sadly Lorna passed away a few years ago but I have never had any thoughts of moving away from here.

I own a cove boat, just under 16 foot. I don't go very far out from the shore. The furthest I go is to the Gwineas buoy so I can still see land. I fish as a hobby; handlining for mackerel, work a couple of crab pots and in the latter part of the year, fish for squid. It's a pleasurable hobby; it's nice out there on your tod floating about watching the world go by.

I have always had a keen interest in railways since I was five years old. My father bought me a train set and I've never looked back. I was a keen train spotter in the times of steam trains and retained an interest in railways and building model locomotives, coaches and layouts. I've always bought a house which can accommodate my railway models. I belong to a local club for railway enthusiasts meeting twice a week.

I have lots in Mevagissey to keep me busy!

ALFIE MACDONALD

FISHERMAN

"Obviously fishing is what I have always wanted to do and what I will do forever to be fair"

When I was younger I used do a lot of rod and line fishing and won quite a few trophies. Then I left school at 16 years old and pretty much got on the big boats from then. I got into fishing going out with my Uncle Jamie on his chartered boat rod and line fishing.

I started fishing on the *Spirited Lady* for a year and now been part of the crew on John Hunkin's boat *Celtic Dawn* for a couple years now and go out for a couple days; longest we can go for has been an eight-day trip. I really enjoy it being out at sea, mainly because it's so calm and peaceful. The winter is always the worst part of the year when you can't go out to sea, then you aren't earning. People never realise how weather or repairs on the boat can stop you going to sea and a chance of catching fish and earning some money. I hate not being able to get out to sea for any reason, because I don't want to do anything else. Hopefully one day I would like to have my own boat, but at the minute I am doing alright with the boat I am on right now.

JAMIE MACDONALD

FISHERMAN & CHARTERED BOAT OWNER

"The next generation might come along and go into fishing but there are so many rules and new regulations making it more difficult. And it's why the Fishermen's Mission is so helpful, when fishermen do need their help"

I worked with Gary Tyler as crew and running his boat the *Lizy*, but I originally started on the boats with Will Shugg and then about ten years ago I bought my own boat 'Isis'. I had worked as a chef before then for many years until my car accident, after which they said that when I worked on the boats, it helped my physio because of the physical work and it allowed me to be flexible in my recovery. Even though if you didn't go out to sea you didn't earn money! So when I got my own boat, I could work it whenever it suited me and I just loved being out on the water.

The *Isis* has just been sold and I have moved over to a chartered boat for angling trips and it's called the *Huntress*. I took the name from Michael Barron's boat called the *Huntress* because he helped me with nets, pointers, and fishing marks. It helped me out when I didn't know too much, even though I had worked on a few boats. I liked him and the name of his boat, hence I am calling this boat after the *Huntress* which will be based in Hayle. I will always carry an 'Albert' collection box (Fishermen's Mission) on board my chartered boat.

HAILEY MACDONALD

FISHERMAN'S DAUGHTER & COASTAL BRIDAL

"I've been in the fishing community all my life, what with my dad and my fiancé of ten years being in fishing. You're at school with children of fishermen and socialise with fishing families and it's simply a way of life for us. It's a lifestyle"

Living and working in Mevagissey, I'm lucky the community supports my local business 'Coastal Bridal' that I've had now for seven years and been something I always wanted to do and couldn't imagine having to work anywhere else. My customers choose to come to my shop because it's in Mevagissey, because it ties in with their own childhood memories; like they create another life's moment. It also spreads business around for restaurants and B&Bs when the bride each time brings six or more relatives and friends with her. It helps in the dead of winter for business.

We did trash a wedding dress when doing some photographs of our dresses on the harbour and one model, Jasmine, jumped into the harbour! The dress came out full of sand, shells and sea weed. The dresses are more robust than people give them credit for and it washed up wonderfully.

GARY TYLER

SKIPPER, FISHERMAN & LEISURE CRUISE BOAT OWNER

"I've been fishing one kind or another all my life."

It started off just with angling with just a rod and reel as a kid. With fishing you are either born into it or you start down the route I did. I'd been to sea a few times and then had my first boat 20-odd year ago called *Trewartha*; a small 20-foot KingFisher20 licensed fishing vessel. I believe it means 'Higher Farm' in Cornish. We caught quite a wide variety of fish all year round. I've always had boats that caught fish!

I'm looking for a smaller fishing vessel now as I have just sold *Trewartha* and I've started out with a glass-bottom boat for leisure cruises. I am now looking for a single-handed fishing vessel at the moment. *Lizy* FH69 was my main fishing vessel for a number of years. That was a big fast boat and with a crew, fishing full-time and caught a lot of fish! The crew were Jamie MacDonald, John Edge and Tim Blamey. You'd be out 1 o'clock in the morning and you would have to keep them fed and watered, back in at 7 o'clock in the evening and gone out again the same time next morning! Day after day; it's very unsocial hours. Fish move in the dim light; they move from A to B at dusk or dawn, so that's why fishermen's hours are so unsocial, so you got all your nets in the water before daylight, then the fish move and you have your catch.

JOHN EDGE

MOBILE FISHMONGER & RETIRED FISHERMAN

"From the age of five or six years old I was always interested in fish. I used to watch the old guys fishing and thought I will have a go at that! So I did! I was a fisherman for 35 years but it was getting tougher going out fishing and now I work for myself as a mobile fishmonger from my van"

My parents moved to Mevagissey when I was younger from Bolton, Lancashire. They moved away again and I came back when I was 18 years old and went fishing. I started with the crew on the *Aquila*, my first boat – the skipper then was Martin Carrington – then fished on the *Jonlee*, and ended up fishing with Tim Blamey on the *Demelza* until I retired five years ago from fishing. There were good days and some scary ones in the bad weather but we always seemed to get through it. I was small-boat fishing rather than on the larger vessels, so would go away a day or two; majority of the time in-shore fishing. We'd catch Dover sole, pollock, bass, and mackerel. We would catch a couple of ton of pollock but there's not so many left now, same with Dover sole which are extremely expensive fish now.

So I started up my own business selling fresh fish from the back of my van 'Mevagissey Bay Fish'. I sell fish at Mevagissey, Lostwithiel, Fowey, Carlyon Bay, St Mawes and Polgooth. I get my fish from whereever I can buy fresh fish from – even the fish market in Plymouth sometimes. People want to buy fresh fish more and more and the fish prices are very high at the moment – highest I have ever known them. The people who like fish will afford fish and it appears to be the older generation 70% of the time that buys fish.

KIM WIGMORE

MEVAGISSEY WET FISH VAN

"Our fish is fresh! It's only known the fridge, and not the freezer. We know the fish's 'birth certificate' here and who caught it!"

The fishing industry had never been anything to do with me until we bought the business 18 years ago and most of the fishermen thought I'd not last three months. Men had tried the business before me and ended up in the pub, instead of running the business. I stick at it from March to New Year's Eve. Women are more stubborn and stick it out.

I love the harbour and love to walk at the end of my working day out to the end of the harbour and just look at it all and think, "God it's beautiful here". It's not ruined and remains as it always has been and that's important. It's an actual fishing village, not over-commercialised like other places in Cornwall. The people are genuine and they haven't spoilt the look of the properties. The actual atmosphere is still a community; we look out for each other here.

I know all the fishermen's comings and goings and I worry over them if they are back late. Things can suddenly go wrong, even when the sea is calm. You don't need a storm for accidents to happen at sea. A freak wave can turn a boat over on a calm sea.

We buy all our fish from Mevagissey fishermen. We know the name of the boat and when it was caught. There is no point being here and not selling fresh fish! The local supermarkets buy from outside of the county, when they have fresh fish right on their doorstep!

OLLIE WIGMORE

FISHERMAN

"I've gone out with my dad (fisherman Russell Wigmore) since I was six years old. I've always loved fishing"

I live in Mevagissey and always wanted to be a fisherman and to be amongst the boats. One day I hope to eventually have my own boat. I love seeing the fish coming through the holder, seeing the crabs to pick out, and the money I can earn and the fresh air and sea.

We start off at 4.30am and could go out for a three- or four-day trip and even eight-day trips sometimes. I enjoy it all. The fishermen all stick together as a family, having some fun and a laugh together. We look after each other and all get along, talking to each other every day. It's very family-based in Mevagissey.

The harbour is my own front yard; I've grown up here amongst it all. When I am home, I come down here every morning and have a coffee and look at each boat in the harbour and talk with the fishermen. The boats are mainly less than ten metres and vary from mackerel boats to netters and trawlers; it's a real mix.

It's a small Cornish fishing village that is working all the time, with boats coming and going out to sea. I was born and bred here and love it.

RUSSELL WIGMORE

FISHERMAN

"Catching pilchards as the sun is coming up; it's just beautiful. There have been a couple times where we've had real near misses, when the boat's nearly gone over when we've been bass fishing; when you are right in tight and the waves break at the wrong time! But that's fishing. You have to take your chances. Everything comes to the back of the boat and the bow of the boat is up in the air!"

I've been fishing with Alan Furse for 22 years. I moved to Mevagissey from Reading and was injured at work on a building site. After a few months off work I went to work with Alan. I used to stand on the wall and Alan asked if I wanted to go out with him. So I did. From then on we've fished together on the *Britannia* and the *Cornishman* and now the *Superb 2*. The *Britannia* is on the mud-flats in Truro now I noticed; she's up and running still.

I enjoy everything about fishing and being with Al; he's a good skipper and bloke to be with and work for. Every day is different going out to sea and you rely on each other and Al taught me everything I know about fishing. We'd go out early in the morning and once we were going out around Caerhays and it was snowing, we were on the *Cornishman* and were absolutely frozen stiff, but when the sun came up it wasn't too bad.

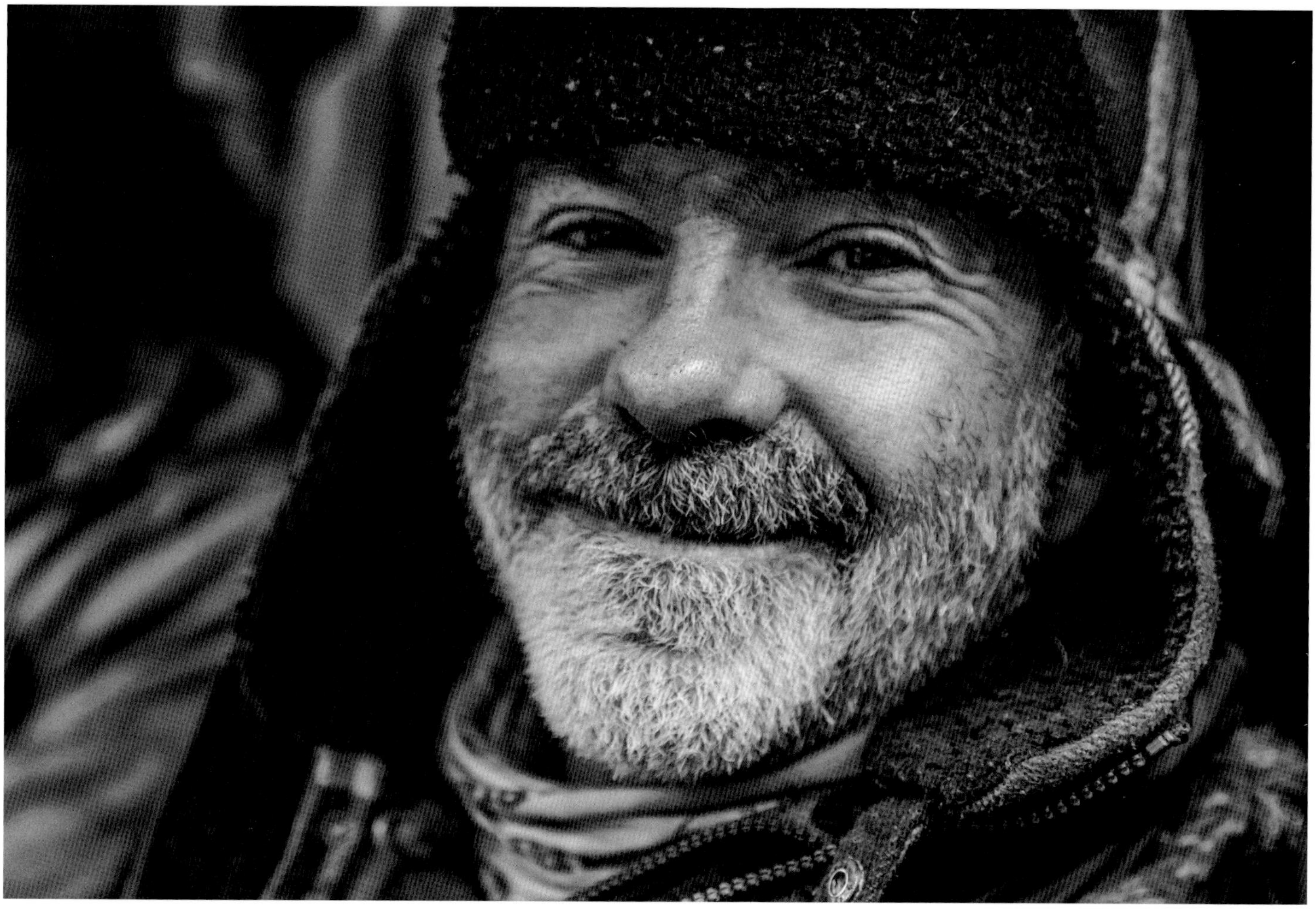

WILLIAM SHUGG

FISHERMAN

"When I was a boy the Lost Gardens of Heligan were still lost!"

I was born in Mevagissey in 1975. Mum and Dad had the leather shop at the bottom of Tregoney Hill called The Beachcomber. I was fishing at the age of five with my Dad and I was allowed to take the boat out on my own at the age of ten. This wouldn't meet safety standards nowadays! It was a very different world back then. We had a lot of freedom growing up in and around Mevagissey. I left school at the age of fifteen to work on the *Britannia IV* with Freddy Turner and Ginge. We were fishing for tuna off the Bay of Biscay. I worked on other boats as crew until I got my own boat the *Radjel* in 2007.

Mevagissey and its harbour are everything to me. My job, my life, my home. The inner and outer harbour make it unique and it's not too big or busy with rich folk's yachts. It's the gateway to getting out to sea and making money. Its where I love to be.

One time I sank in Lantic Bay and the Mevagissey fishermen came to re-float the boat and bring it home. This shows the great sense of community spirit. I was four months on the slip at the height of the season making good the boat. I became a tourist attraction. A lady on holiday asked me why it was taking so long. I told her, "It's people like you, keep asking me questions!"

I am currently involved in a cetacean mitigation. It's a three-year study and the aim is to find ways to fish without catching any dolphins and to ease their suffering. This involves live video recording of nets coming aboard, acoustic 'pingers' that emit a noise the dolphins shy away from, lights on the strings of nets and shorter soak times. There is no other place in the world I would rather be and no other job or way of life that I would rather live.

ANDY MINGO

FISHERMAN

"I still have that burning passion I had as a kid about fishing; I've always been fascinated with the fish. I've gotten softer as I got older; I'd rather not kill 'em. Wish I could make a living by taking a picture and letting 'em go. I don't like to harm anything I don't have to!"

I started fishing when I was 13; at weekends and holidays and any bit of spare time I had really. As a nipper I was just fascinated with what came out from the sea. Me and William Shugg were always around the harbour. We'd go in the angling shop, Dick would give us a bit of tackle, then we'd go get some bait and not part with a penny and end out the quay fishing.

I knocked around the harbour as a nipper and it was natural. I'd go and do it. I left school early and went crabbing and netting with Andrew Trevarton (second cousins), and mackerel on the hooks; that was good, enjoyed that. His father Frank Trevarton taught me the trade; I was a bit of a tearaway when I was younger and he wanted me to calm down and toe the line like. But Frank was very patient and he taught me everything I know really.

I'm getting older and stiffer in the joints, but still got a few years in me yet! If you got the sun on your back working away, you wouldn't want to be anywhere better. Another day and wished I'd paid better attention in school. But you are a bit of a free spirit when you're fishing; it's your life. I work with Chris Blamey now for the past five years.

CHRIS BLAMEY

SKIPPER OF GALWAD-Y-MOR

"I was sat talking to the boat-builder one day and he simply said 'you can go anywhere in the world but you'll never find a place as nice to live as Mevagissey'. I decided there and then he was right!"

Blameys have fished for hundreds of years here but my father felt he didn't want his children in the fishing industry and wanted us to have alternative options. So I went off to Camborne School of Mines and did geology. I worked in a gold mine in Northern Ireland after graduating, but always looking for a job in Cornwall. I came to a realisation then that I was really happy in Mevagissey and focused on the fishing. I used to say to my Dad, "I can put up with either bad weather or bad fishing but not at the same time!"

I am skipper on my father's boat, *Galwad-Y-Mor* (Cornish for 'Call of the Sea') and been fishing for ten years now. I had always worked during my holidays and weekends with my father, so it wasn't like a massive change. We have done a lot of fishing in this time and focused on earning everyone a living; it's a permanent pressure. Dad is still going to sea, he takes the smaller boat to sea and we still work together with the ring netting during the winter, with two boats. I shoot the net around the fish and he comes over to me and picks up the tow rope and he can keep me from getting tangled up in the net!

PETER BLAMEY

FISHERMAN

"Boats are always female. If you look after them, they will look after you"

"I was born in the village in a house on Polkirt Hill where I lived for over 20 years. The beam of the lighthouse would shine on my bedroom wall.

I left school at 15 and went into fishing. In the 1970s there was plenty of fish, although it was quantity as opposed to quality. In the summer months I used to do angling trips for shark fishing.

My present boat, the *Galwad-Y-Mor*, which means 'Call of the Sea', is a wooden boat which was built in 1984 in the local boatyard in Mevagissey. I've owned wooden boats all my life."

Peter has recently bought another boat, *Girl Rachel*, which is a fibreglass boat which was also built in 1984 in Rock near Padstow. His son Chris prefers the fibreglass boat as it requires less maintenance.

Chris was the only one of Peter's three children who went into fishing. After gaining a degree in exploration geology at Exeter University, he took some time out to decide his career path. However, he needed to raise some funds and so decided to join his father fishing, as an interim plan. Peter was ring netting at the time. He bought his son some oilskins and he took to the sea. Chris actually found fishing 'quite exciting' and has now been fishing for ten years!

"I am a Harbour Trustee. There are ten of us including the Harbour Master. We have a few grants which enable us to do repairs on the quay and carry out essential maintenance. The fish store is run as a separate entity. One of the reasons Mevagissey harbour is so successful is the fact we have good fish store facilities including fridges and ice machines. We have between 40 and 50 fishermen who pay into the running of the West Quay facilities.

I'm very attached to Mevagissey harbour. If I go up to London for a trip, I can't wait to get back home!"

PENNY BLAMEY

FISHERMAN'S WIFE

"Stood at the landing window of the house on Polkirt Hill waiting to see the boat come into port, no communications at all then. How scary!"

Moving to Mevagissey in 1983 from a Lincolnshire market town, I was viewed with curiosity and a degree of suspicion by locals – an 'incomer'! But I loved life here. Peter and I met in 1984 and when we married a year later, I knew that I would spend the rest of my life here. Our children followed: Ben in 1987, Rebecca in 1989 and Christopher in 1991. Life as a fisherman's wife was quite a challenge, often on my own for days at a time, with three under-fives! There was little time to worry. I just got on with it!

Communication with the boat was sketchy; a coded message via my father-in-law's radio when they were a couple of hours away, often after no news for days. Later came the (expensive) satellite phone for emergencies, then better mobile coverage happened.

I often think of my late mother-in-law having her husband and both sons on one boat, telling me how she stood at the landing window of the house on Polkirt Hill waiting to see the boat come into port, no communications at all then. How scary!

I am so thankful that my lovely daughter-in-law and her generation, whilst still having the anxieties that go with being the wife of a fisherman, have the reassurance of all the technology in both communications and safety equipment that make life at sea a little easier now. The scary stuff is still there, but this is not a job, it is a way of life and that will never change.

JONATHAN BARRON RIP

"Grandfather lived in 'The Cuddy', Polkirt Hill, and saw a child drowning! He jumped over the wall, slid down the cliff-face and dived into the harbour to rescue the boy. Grandfather was awarded a bravery medal. He rescued two other children, but declined any further awards or acknowledgement"

This experience led Jonathan's grandfather to teach his children and grandchildren to swim. "Grandfather would pay us a penny for swimming from the slipway to Sandy Beach; a half a crown if we swam the 'pool' (across the harbour)." Jonathan explained that every eldest son of a Barron born in Mevagissey was named Jonathan, a recorded fact dating from 1730, and were all connected to the fishing industry of Mevagissey. His own father, Jonathan, who was a strong swimmer, was unable to fish, due to his 'dilated heart' from catching a chill, swimming. Instead he became an antique seller.

"Grandfather Jonathan Barron had started fishing when he was ten years old. He eventually owned a lugger called The Foam. He became Fishing Officer for Mevagissey harbour for 20 years, and was selected from 98 applicants for the position as Cornwall's Fisheries Officer in 1910. He was awarded the MBE for 20 years' services to Cornwall's Fisheries, by King George V. Grandfather was worried what to wear to meet King George V, but received a letter from the Lord Chamberlain at St James' Palace reassuring him, that 'his semi-naval uniform as Fisheries Officer was fine and permissible to wear to meet the King.'

Grandfather attended a court case in London, to give evidence against a ship trying to sell 'Norwegian sprats as sardines!' The family owns a leather-bound book, full of newspaper cuttings, all related to Cornwall's fishing over his 60-year career. "Grandfather's only daughter Winifred, known as 'Ifford', was the last fishing woman in Mevagissey: a spinster, who fished on her own."

DAVID 'TREACLE' TREGALE

FISHERMAN

"Neither my father or grandfather could swim!"

"I am a Mevagissey boy from a fishing family. My grandfather James Hunkin was a fisherman all his life. Me and my friend bought the boat called the *Ibis* when we left school and I've done part-time fishing for about 40 years. Now that I have left work, I fish full-time. In 2005 I bought my friend's boat which was called *Wave 2*. I didn't like the name so I managed to re-register it as *Verona* which was the name of my grandfather's boat: a Plymouth Pilot, a fibreglass boat. I fish for bass, mackerel and squid, all lines, no nets."

David is known fondly around the harbour as 'Treacle'. Apparently, he can be quite accident-prone, spilling things and, living up to his name, he had a near-fatal accident a few months ago which nearly cost his life.

"This year, in the summer, I fell off the boat and nearly drowned. I had moored up in the outer harbour. I'd finished for the day. I picked up the rope next to the boat, went up on the deck and slipped off. I fell into the water."

Fortunately for David, another fisherman, Colin Williams, was close by and was able to bring him over to the slip. A member of the harbour staff recalled how, when they brought him onto land, he seemed lifeless but with some quick thinking and first aid he regained consciousness and lived to tell the tale! He admits that neither he nor his father or grandfather – all fishermen – could swim.

"It was scary. I was very lucky and I wear my lifejacket all the time now."

SUSAN TREGALE

FISHERMAN'S WIFE & ARTIST

"He does things the Cornish way, dreckly"

Susan's bubbly and forthright character has helped her deal with the challenges of being a fisherman's wife. Susan has been married to David Tregale (Treacle) for 45 years and by her own admission, being a fisherman's wife is not easy. She describes her husband as someone who does things the Cornish way. In other words: 'dreckly'.

As well as working, Susan is an accomplished artist. Her works include stunning paintings of seascapes, coastal views and tin mines of Cornwall. She sells and exhibits her work locally. Often, she can be seen walking her beautiful German Shepherd, Sasha, in and around the village.

She jokingly said that being married to a fisherman is a bit like being a widow, which was almost the case as she recalls the incident back in the summer, when David almost drowned after falling overboard from his boat in the harbour.

"I told him one day it would happen, he would fall overboard! He can't swim, just like his father and grandfather! He will wear his lifejacket all the time from now on!"

COLIN 'FISHY' WILLIAMS

RETIRED FISHERMAN

"Probably the prettiest, most natural kind of Cornish fishing port still intact that you could see: quintessential Cornwall"

Colin, or Fishy as he is known by his fellow fishermen, grew up "a few miles up the road from Mevagissey". As a boy of 16 he went fishing with different boats until at 18 he bought his own boat, a tosher, catching mackerel and doing inshore trawling. In the 1960s following a short time in Lowestoft where he joined a trawler and fished in the North Sea, he went on to do a teacher training course. "As a teacher, I continued to fish part-time, and realised I could make more money fishing than teaching! I gave up teaching and went to France where I bought a trawler which I brought back to Mevagissey and modernised. At one stage I had a small fleet of boats here.

In the 1970s thousands of tons of mackerel were being caught off the coast of Cornwall by local boats. On one occasion, on a calm, still day off the Lizard, I came across a huge 1000-ton Russian trawler. The crew had lowered small boats and were painting the rust patches. It was a factory boat canning mackerel. A Jacob's ladder hung down, my crewman came alongside and I climbed up to be met by what looked like a member of the KGB who was not happy at my arrival! However, the Captain appeared who welcomed me. I described Mevagissey to him and he said that he had come from a very similar place on the Black Sea. I told him I knew the waters well and would give him information about wrecks if he in return would give me his knowledge. He willingly did this and I passed the information on to The Admiralty and to the Hydrographic Office. They then sent boats to locate the wrecks but didn't find one! However, even now those wrecks are still marked on the printouts!"

Colin is happy that Mevagissey continues to be a thriving port and continues to attract young men into the industry.

KAREN KESSI NÉE WILLIAMS

DAUGHTER OF COLIN 'FISHY' WILLIAMS

I grew up with the smell of salt and seaweed and harbour mud on the sunny side and remember running upstairs to lean out the window, scanning the bay for Dad's boat when Mum called, "He's coming in!" Then I was off down the slip and out to the quay to watch him land. Trailing fish guts and seagulls like feast week decorations, great big boxes full of slippery cod, hake, whiting, lemon sole, plaice and all the rest being heaved up on to the quay, with tourists getting in the way, eager to have a closer look; Dad yelling, "Stand back!"

On good days, I was allowed to clamber down on deck and hunt for treasures, as long as I was careful not to get in the way: starfish, coral, big delicate fan shells and razor clams, even the occasional goose barnacle looking like something from a 1970s alien film. When he was scallop dredging, the treat was to be sitting perched on a big bag of scallops and eating one that Dad opened for me straight from the shell, sweet and still tasting of sea. That was the best bit, really, of being a fisherman's child. We ate so well, even in the days before the money was good, dining on crab, lobster, crayfish, turbot and monkfish all year round. The worst were the long winter nights when I crept in to curl up next to Mum as the wind howled and we pretended not to be worried that he was out there in the dark stormy channel.

SHIRLEY & THE LATE PETER RANDALL

"You can't take the village girl to a city but you can take the city boy to a small village"

Shirley Randall (Hunkin) was born in Mevagissey. Her early memories were of helping her gran and grandad in Edwards, the fishmonger's shop, to prepare the crab in the back room for sandwiches which they sold. "There's nothing quite like hot, fresh crab when it comes straight out of the boiler! As a child I remember going into the salt cellars below what is now the Wheelhouse, where they had the pilchard presses which was where my gran worked. My father worked in the cannery as a packer. As children all we knew were the beaches and we spent all our spare time swimming off Sandy Beach and Island Quay." Shirley was working in the chemist in the village when she met Peter. Unlike Shirley, Peter was a Plymouth boy. He would visit Mevagissey, often the Ship Inn, with his friends and it was on one of these occasions that they met. A few months later, Shirley moved up to Plymouth to live initially with a girl friend and then with Peter's mother so she could be nearer to him. "Peter at this time was working on the trawlers and would often be out at sea for up to 72 hours at a time so I wouldn't see him. I hated being in Plymouth and so after six months I returned with Peter to Mevagissey. You can't take the village girl to a city but you can take the city boy to a small village."

For a while he went back on the trawlers working with some of the local fishermen. He was an engineer by trade; his skills of splicing ropes and mending nets were excellent! Peter secured a mooring in Mevagissey Harbour. "We owned a tosher called the *Susan Jane* and Peter spent his time fishing and in the summer months would take out day trippers."

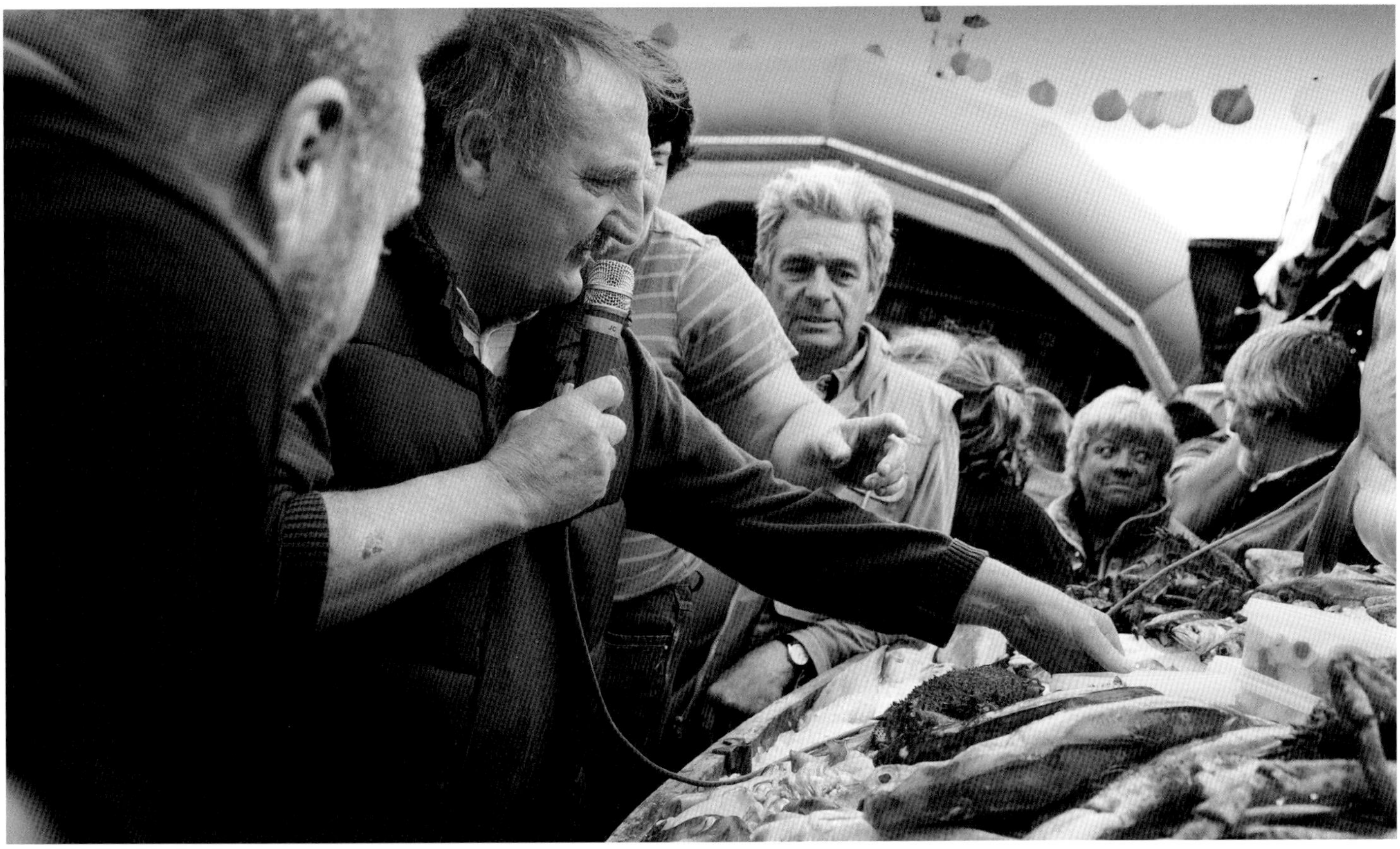

In his early 40s Peter started up his fish round where he became fondly known as 'Pete The Fish'. He had many regular customers; some would give him a key so when he had delivered the fish he could go in and make himself a cup of tea and some even left him a meal to heat up in the microwave! "I used to get up early to make him sandwiches but could never understand why he hadn't eaten them!" Peter used to buy the fish from the Barbican in Plymouth as well as from the harbour. On one occasion when he bought a box of fish in Plymouth, under the fish, at the bottom of the box, was a massive oyster. "There was no pearl inside, typical Randall luck!" It turned out to be the biggest oyster found in Cornish seas and even led him to be interviewed on national TV! He donated the oyster to the Aquarium.

Peter was such a great character and would always have a funny tale to tell. He was quite accident-prone. "Once, while cleaning the deck, he fell overboard and emerged still holding the broom in one hand and his fag in the other. There was also the time when he came to visit me in the maternity hospital after our daughter was born looking like a blue smurf! He had been painting the boat on Sandy Beach when he knocked the whole pot of blue paint over him. Despite scrubbing and washing, the blue was difficult to remove. There was also the time when he was driving the van onto the quay and the engine started smoking. Before long it had gone up in flames and had rolled into the old Post Office. He was of course teased afterwards as having 'smoked fish'."

Sadly, due to ill-health Peter had to give up the fish round which he loved. A few years later he joined the museum where he was in his element. He entertained the visitors with his stories, his true stories, and many would write to the Museum mentioning Peter and their visit with great fondness.

Every Feast Week Sunday, Peter would be in charge of the fish auction, and what a great job he would do! Even if you didn't want to buy the fish, he was so entertaining with his banter. He always raised a huge sum of money.

When Peter passed away in 2016, the harbour was lined with hundreds of people, he was a well-loved member of the community. It was his wish that half the money collected at his funeral be given to the Fishermen's Mission.

MEVAGISSEY MUSEUM

"The person that created Pears® soap was from Mevagissey, and Clark Gable was filmed there in 1956. There are lots of things related to farming, fishing and about locals and their history" ***(Visitor Book Aug 2019)***

The building that houses the museum is a museum piece in its own right. Dating from 1745, it was part of a boat builder's yard that at one time extended to the far corner of the cliff. It was built straight into the rock face that you can see behind the kitchen dresser. When it was first built, boats were constructed on the ground floor, while the first floor was the carpenter's workshop and the top floor was used as a store. As the boatyard became more successful the yard expanded outwards and was a hive of activity for many years. When the last boat builder to work in this building, Arthur Frazier, retired, he kindly offered to sell the building to the museum at a reduced cost and thanks to the generosity of a local benefactor, Mrs Matson, the museum trustees were able to acquire the building for future generations.

There is a wonderful collection of photographs depicting village life in the 19th and 20th century, as well as many other small and larger exhibits, including the Andrew Pears story.

The museum is run by volunteers and has free entrance. Visitors of all ages regularly show their appreciation with donations which are very welcome.

From left: Chris, Steve, Paul and Mike

MEVAGISSEY FERRY, BESSIE JAMES

"Bessie James carries up to 50 passengers between the quaint historic ports of Mevagissey and Fowey, departing from the Lighthouse Quay in Mevagissey every morning at ten. The service starts in late spring until the close of season in October"

The ferry is moored in the outer harbour and easily found as a familiar red-and-white vessel, bedecked in bunting and banners advertising her two much-loved destinations of Mevagissey and Fowey. Every day the skipper studies the weather forecasts and sea, knowing that just one mile per hour over his wind speed limits can make the difference between smiles or a greenish tinge round the gills for passengers! It's definitely a weather-dependent service and the winds and swell may dictate a cancellation; there is a well known local lore, "If the ferry int runnin, you dun' wanna be out there."

The crew always goes out of their way to give passengers the added pleasure of seeing dolphins, porpoises, diving gannets, the occasional fin whale, sun fish, seals and a variety of sea birds during their trip. Locals and visitors year after year look forward to enjoying a car-free day out while enjoying the Cornwall coastline, the sea and fresh air, travelling between the two historic Cornish ports.

RNLI MEVAGISSEY

VOLUNTEERS

"It is so important that our shop continues to raise money for the RNLI, the charity that saves lives at sea"

The Mevagissey RNLI shop opened in 1932, initially in Church Street. It continues to thrive and generate a large amount of money annually for the charity. The success is down to the volunteers who can be seen running stalls at many events within the village including Mevagissey Feast Week. Their stall was also present when royalty, Prince Charles, visited three years ago. He showed a supportive and genuine interest in all that the RNLI does in Mevagissey and Gorran.

Often in the summer the lifeboat visits once or twice from Fowey to the excitement of tourists, adults and children alike, who are invited to climb aboard this wonderful boat, a vessel of paramount importance to saving lives off our shores. During Mevagissey Feast Week, the RNLI boat puts on a display in the bay demonstrating a sea rescue and onlookers can see at first hand the challenges that can be faced.

The shop relies totally on volunteers and opens during school holidays and through the summer months.

SARAH MACANDREW

MEVAGISSEY STORES

"The fishing families of Mevagissey are a massive support to my shop. They shop here, they buy here, they are my customers; they are my bread and butter. We work together; I need them as much as they need me. And sometimes there are some special smells! 'Oh, you've been fishing today?' as if we need to ask!"

I am always happy to support the Fishermen's Mission charity anytime, because they've helped out loads of families locally in the fishing community. Anything that helps families locally I will get behind and support too. We know the fishing industry is volatile; it's not a guaranteed income. The fishing folk are good people and they are loyal, hardworking and real characters.

They are a strong community that support each other and I try and provide the best service I can to them all – it's a personal business that I do my best to keep up services for them and running it the best I can. It's a life-line for some people who can't leave the village and need a store of convenience that I try to offer with the shop, Post Office and cash ATM.

Mevagissey is so lucky that it is still a busy fishing harbour, compared with other Cornish coastal towns and villages where the population has fallen, but we are still an 'all-year-round' fishing village, so I have 'all-year -round' customers.

MEVAGISSEY GIG CLUB

"Strong competition on the water, and a great social event, with a touch of singing"

We are one of the oldest gig rowing clubs in Cornwall, established in 1986 and a founder member of the Cornish Pilot Gig Association. We are the proud owners of four beautiful Cornish pilot gigs and a giglet: The fleet consist of three wooden gigs, *Elowen*, *Lannvorek* and *Endeavour* and a fibreglass gig called *Silver Fox*, named after Martin Walton the backbone of the club. Finally, the giglet an 18-foot four-seated Cornish gig, designed by Gary Mitchell of Portmellon. In the last 35 years, the clubs base has seen us move from Mevagissey Social Club, to John Moore's boat yard, Mevagissey and finally come to rest at Portmellon Cove; just a stone's throw from Mevagissey.

Throughout the summer months, we row Mondays, Wednesday and Thursdays and compete at the weekends at various places throughout Cornwall and the South West, with the winter months rowing on a Sunday morning, when the weather permits. We are made up of ladies' crews, juniors and men's crews, with diverse ages from 11 to 73 years of age. The rowing club has ventured far and wide, competing in the World Pilot Gig Championships on the Isles of Scilly, France, Holland, Faroe Islands, Boston USA and locally throughout the South West. It's also been great to see our rowers achieve some amazing feats, such as rowing unaided 3000 miles across the Atlantic Ocean, or 360 miles around Cornwall, or an open row to Tresco, on the Isles of Scilly.

ALICE FOARD

"My father, David, and uncle, Peter Foard, were born at home in Cross Park Terrace in 1931; the first twins, I am told, to survive in Mevagissey for many years. Despite their father's death when they were six, their life, along with their elder brother Ron's, was full of fun, mischief and high jinks!"

Their mother ran D L Foard's; the grocer's at the bottom of School Hill. They managed to gain entrance to grammar school, leaving at 14 for their apprenticeship with Percy Mitchell's boatyard. This gave them the foundations for travelling around the world teaching their skills.

Peter travelled the world – Europe, Canada, Conakry (West Africa) Sri Lanka and Indonesia – where the sun hat he wore crossed the equator "more times than you've had hot dinners!" Dad, married with two children, travelled to Sri Lanka and Indonesia teaching and surveying boats, six weeks home, six weeks away. But both men always returned home to Mevagissey.

Dad worked within the fishing industry surveying boats, and Peter began building boats again down Portmellon. Both men were instrumental in the formation of the Choir – Geoff Pollard wrote a song on how Peter would harass him every time they met – and were immensely proud of its achievements, and again travelled to many parts of the globe with them. In the 80s they both embarked on getting Mevagissey a gig club. David organising and Peter (with Tom Dudley) building their first boat the *Endeavour.*

Mevagissey was certainly their home that they were immensely proud of; and the world was there to be seen and enjoyed.

DAVID & DOLORES PALK

"We sat together in the front row at school"

David and Dolores were both born in Mevagissey, sat at the same desk at school, have been married for 52 years and have fond memories of their childhood in the village.

However, there has been a history of tragedy in Dolores' family of fishermen. "In 1948, my grandfather, John F Hunkin was lost overboard at the age of 58. Then eleven years later his brother, Richard Hunkin, was also lost at sea. Both of them have plaques in their memory in the Fishermen's Mission building in Penryn."

David's grandfather was a boatbuilder and worked in Mitchell's boatyard in Portmellon. "I was a train driver for a time and then went into engineering, had my own business and did that 'til I retired. I was involved in the Mevagissey museum for 25 years." One of the fondest memories for them both was the restoration of the Wesleyan Church Banner.

"David and I remember a couple coming into the museum. They had found a rolled-up banner in the garage of a property they had bought: it was in a terrible state. I recognised that it had come from the Wesleyan Chapel. I used to belong to the chapel and when I was about 12, I remember carrying this banner during Feast Week with my friend Sylvia Gascoigne. We researched how we could have it restored and the museum had the work carried out, accessing a grant from the Pilgrim Trust and Heritage Lottery. The project was called 'Flying the Flag'. It was returned in 2017. We then had it framed and it now hangs in pride of place in the museum."

LORNA CAVANAGH & MARILYN WINGFIELD

FISHERMAN'S DAUGHTERS

Lorna: "I realised I was related to two-thirds of the class in my school. It used to upset me that I might not find anyone to get married to!"

Sisters Marilyn and Lorna, and their brother Geoff (Pollard), were born and bred in Mevagissey in No. 4 Bank Terrace. The fishermen in their family go back as far as the 1500s! Lorna remembers going out in the boat with her dad when she was young. "I used to get up at four in the morning so I could go out fishing with him. I loved it, especially feathering. In those days there was no fishing allowed on a Sunday. A chain was put across from Lighthouse Quay to East Quay to prevent boats from leaving the harbour."

Marilyn wasn't so keen on fishing, but instead enjoyed going to the beach. "Dad didn't have a car so he would take us from Mevagissey to Gorran Haven in the boat. We would jump off, swim into the beach, spend the day there and he would pick us up when he had finished fishing.

Our mum worked in one of the bakeries. She was the first woman in Mevagissey to have a driving licence, which she needed in order to drive the delivery van!"

After her husband passed away, Lorna moved across the road at Bank Terrace to live with Marilyn in the house their father had built in 1963, a house which has always stayed in the family. "Dad used to make and repair his nets in the part of the house downstairs that was used for storage."

Marilyn and Lorna loved growing up in Mevagissey and describe it as being a wonderful childhood. Although Lorna's son and family live in New Zealand, her daughter and Marilyn's three daughters have their own families who continue to live and enjoy Cornish Life!

MEVAGISSEY BAY
Geoff Pollard

GEOFF POLLARD

RETIRED CARPENTER, MUSICIAN & SONGWRITER

"Living a musical life beside the sea has been a privilege"

"Until age 15, I assumed I would fish. Dad worked on the *Ibis* alongside cousins the Lakeman brothers. Built by uncle Percy Mitchell at Portmellon she was a strong, capable boat fit for most weathers. By 1958, boats were disappearing from the harbour. Family boats such as *Vera*, *Seagull*, *Margaret* and eventually *Ibis*, went. Fishermen were buying smaller boats or retiring. Things looked grim for school-leavers like me. Most of my friends got jobs ashore in the china clay industry or building, with me a carpenter.

By 1968, the contraction prompted the Mevagissey Museum to form to preserve local artefacts. My dad was a founder member before passing in 1985. Later, the curator John Clayton invited me to replace Dad on the committee, and I eventually became a trustee.

Music was always important to my family. In 1974, pressure was exerted on Percy's son Gary and me to form a male choir akin to Treviscoe and Marazion. Peter Foard persisted until we gathered in November 1974, eventually forming Mevagissey Male Choir. I was a member for 40 years although abroad for some of that time.

For me music involved singing, arranging and writing, in my youth listening to the Octet, around the Congregational Chapel and latterly singing with the Mevagissey 6 and Meva 4. Many family members engaged, with pianist cousin Brian accompanying the Male Choir.

I only started writing music seriously leading up to Peter Foard's Memorial Concert, penning a couple of songs which seemed to be well received. My songs align with my memories of local places and events.

My current choir, Imerys Mid-Cornwall Choir, has recently reconvened since Covid. Only after several weeks' rehearsal has my voice returned."

Geoff is very modest when it comes to his musical achievements. He composed a song 'Mevagissey Bay' for the Mevagissey Male Choir, for whom he was a founder member. Sung as a solo and then accompanied by the choir, it is arguably one of the most beautiful songs that they sing. The lyrics about our beautiful village often bring a tear to the eye of those listening.

"None of us knows what the future will bring. Living a musical life beside the sea has been a privilege especially when shared with strong family and friends."

GARY MITCHELL

BOAT DESIGNER

Mevagissey and Portmellon have quite a history of boatbuilding. The principal builders dating back to the 1700s were Shepherd, Dunn, Lelean, Frazier and Roberts. Apart from fishing boats of various sizes, large sailing cargo vessels up to 110 feet long were built in both Mevagissey and Portmellon. Some of the larger vessels carried pilchards to Italy. My father George Percy Mitchell was a part of that tradition. He was born at 21 The Cliff, Mevagissey and having left school at the age of 14, he became an indentured apprentice to Henry Roberts, a local boat builder, completed at the age of 21, and he became self-employed. After starting in a small workshop in an old pilchard cellar in Chapel Street, he eventually moved his premises to the south side of Portmellon in 1924, developing a reputation for high quality work. Instead of the popular method of working off a scale model, he self-taught designing boats onto paper.

Over the years he built crafts of all shapes and sizes, from fishing boats, ferries and launches up to large yachts. One yacht he built in 1936 was owned by the sailing master to King George IV, which resulted in our present Queen Elizabeth II sailing on it as a young teenager. After building over 300 boats, he retired in 1967 and my brother Brian and I succeeded him in carrying on the tradition.

I am John Gary Mitchell, Percy Mitchell's youngest son and I became a partner in the yard after having served an apprenticeship with a boat design company in Poole, Dorset. Together with my brother, we built many vessels to my design. I designed my first fibreglass 32-foot fishing boat in 1972 for Cygnus Marine Ltd of Falmouth which led to thousands of boats of all sizes selling throughout the UK and the world. Now at the age of 78, I am still in demand for designs for the UK, Norway, Poland and Africa. I don't see the need to fully retire, so I will carry on and who knows what the future will bring?

PETER MOOR

MEVAGISSEY BOAT BUILDER & REPAIRER

"Of all the fine boats I have worked on, I love to work for the Mevagissey folk the most; it means far more to me"

Peter grew up building boats, learning all the skills and crafts of building a wooden sailing boat or fishing boat from his father John Moor, who is now 87 years old and works part-time. They are both boat builders of renowned reputation too. Each boat designed begins as a small to-scale model of the boat in 3D, for the customer to view their eventual boat. "You can have it all computerised these days, but I still like doing these samples for the customer - to see the finished line and angles of the final product."

All around the eaves of the attic in the boatyard are wooden samples of all the boats Peter and his dad have made over the years: pieces of art in themselves. Peter can look out from his yard to most boats in the harbour and give their history and the owners he knows well.

Peter was repairing a damaged gig from Cadgwith, called the *Socoa*, and he said, "Funnily enough my great-grandparents who came from Cadgwith, remembered when the original *Socoa* was beached in Cadgwith Cove. All the cement in barrels heading for San Francisco (1906) was ditched, but it's funny how a full dinner service found its way onto grandfather's crabber! Great-grandmother loved that dinner service!"

JOHN MOOR

RETIRED BOAT BUILDER

"In 1944, I went to see a film called Johnny Frenchman and saw my life right in front of me!"

"I was an ordinary country boy, the son of a naval man. During the war we lived in Devonport, but when the bombing became bad and my father was away, we moved to Cadgwith.

In 1944, I went to see the film, 'Johnny Frenchman' and saw my life, unbeknown to me then, appear right in front of my eyes." Little did John know then, that he was in fact going to be working in the same boatyard and live in the house where the film was set!

"I came to work in Mitchell's boatyard at Portmellon as an apprentice but after two years went into the air force and following that worked on big ships in the dockyard. Following a short time working in the clay works, something I didn't like, I decided to build a boat in the field at the top of the hill opposite the cemetery. When it was finished, it was sold and went to Padstow. I then went on to work in Charlestown for ten years.

In 1976, I bought the boatyard and house that featured in the film 'Johnny Frenchman'! I have been here ever since. My son, Peter, now runs the boatyard, building small boats. We arrived here in 1976 and built the business up to what it is today."

COLIN HARRIS

THE WATCH HOUSE

I came to Mevagissey in 2004 and saw this wonderful house which was in need of restoration, so that's what I did, and now it is a lovely place to live. I was brought up in Jersey and lived and worked in many places in my career as a chartered accountant, before settling here in Mevagissey.

The Watch House is a strange house in that it 'walks up the cliff'; it is in fact built into the rock. It has a studio at the top which has far-reaching views over the sea. Film companies have used the house for filming at least seven times since I have lived here and it has been fun watching the actors and actresses performing but also during breaks having the opportunity to chat with them about their work. On the last occasion, it was a German company filming a series based on one of the books of Rosamunde Pilcher. In fact, they took over every room of the house which meant I had to move out to a hotel for a couple of days! I think although the filming often gives an idealistic view of the harbour and Mevagissey, it is a great advertisement for the village. We do have a large number of German visitors who come because of the series. They often recognise the boats and the houses featured in the programmes.

It is believed that the Watch House, which is over 300 years old, was so named as it was some kind of customs house. The rooms have very tall ceilings. In fact a photograph in the 1860s shows doors which resemble those of a boat shed and therefore there was possibly a customs boat in here. They wanted to catch people smuggling so they would push the boat down the slip just outside the house and try and catch the offenders. The top room was used as a lookout: a watch station. Although the present studio room is only about 100 years old, there would have been some kind of room there before it was reconstructed.

Over the years I have slowly integrated into the community and a few years ago was asked to be a Harbour Trustee. The Harbour is actually owned by a trust which manages the harbour on behalf of the people of Mevagissey. At times it has been hard work but also very interesting. I am very pleased I settled in Mevagissey.

DAVID WESTON

ARTIST

"I have spotted my painting of 'The Watch House' through people's windows as I pass by and thought: 'Oh that's nice!'"

"We moved to Mevagissey in 1969 and I started a pottery and painting gallery off West Wharf. Sadly, last year they knocked down the premises that I was in, which was originally built as a coal shed. I had a view over the harbour and could watch my little boat moored in the harbour bobbing on the water. I enjoyed closing my pottery and getting out in my little boat. It was magical times to move to Mevagissey and start my career as an artist. It was my initial association with the harbour and my source of inspiration. I ran the pottery for around 11 years and the business was thriving, and opened till late at night most days in the summer. Mevagissey Museum has a couple of examples of my pottery on exhibition."

David Weston Art Gallery sits neatly in St Georges Square, Mevagissey and his popular style of wonderful artwork reflecting Mevagissey is hugely popular and admired. He has displayed his artwork there for the last 50 years. It is a tiny premises with limited space, which restricts the size of his artwork on show. David says "A picture paints a thousand words." His painting of The Watch House on the harbour is a popular watercolour print which has sold in its thousands. He has worked in various mediums and styles and his signature is a little fish.

"I have always been so enthralled by Mevagissey Harbour, rain or shine, standing on Cliff Street with its nucleus remaining the same throughout time."

RUPERT EDWARDES RIP

FISHERMAN

"Meva is still busy and vibrant"

I was born to an army family in Singapore and moved to North Cornwall as a baby. At seven years of age I boarded in Bude and school holidays were spent in Malaya, India, Borneo, Germany and various army destinations. In 1973 I took a berth trawling in Plymouth and then moved on to Fowey. In 1983 I moved to Mevagissey where I loved the place, the people and the local fishing industry. When trawling was slack, we migrated between Brixham and Newlyn and enjoyed meeting other fishermen.

We are lucky in Meva to have a generation of young fishermen combined with generations of knowledge and experience which keeps the village with a purpose and identity outside tourism.

I gave up trawling at 60 and have worked for the last six years on an open 20-foot Treeve boat SS270 with a few hooks, which just about keeps body and soul in order!

Meva is still busy and vibrant and the beer still flows! It's a good life and long may it continue.

MALCOLM SAUNDERS

FISHERMAN

"I've fished my whole life, ever since I can remember! My life history is fishing, fishing, fishing!"

As boys Father took us out every weekend in his little boat fishing. He always wanted to be a fisherman, but my grandmother wouldn't let him. It was when Father died and Mother had no income because she was caring for us; Mother said, "There's no more pocket money." So at 11 years old and my brother 16 years old we caught mackerel on Pentewan beach and sold them at three pence each at Pentewan campsite from a wooden box. We got our pocket money and started our fishing careers. But that is what we did as boys, selling fish. Then we knew everyone in Pentewan, not now, it's all second homes! When I left school I went fishing with the Elvins family in their boat the *Erin*. It was an old lugger, with no wheelhouse, real old boat.

There was a huge fishing fleet here when I started and it's dwindled away. I had to join bigger crews for twenty years, on Spanish longliners, in Holland; all over the North Atlantic, every form of fishing you can name I have done. In my twilight years, I have come back to Mevagissey to catch lobsters in my small 20-foot boat, called *Morgelyn,* enjoying life again.

Course now I am now the new celebrity of Mevagissey since I starred on 'Cornwall: This Fishing Life.' People stop me, "Oh we've seen you on TV" and ask me for a selfie. I am now waiting to go to Hollywood! I could have been starring in 'Pirates of the Caribbean' without even trying. Just being myself. But my life history is fishing, fishing, fishing.

THE KING'S ARMS

KRIS & HELEN NATHAN

"We are so happy we landed here"

Kris and I moved to Mevagissey on 1st October 2014 with our then 18-month-old son Alfred and we reopened The King's Arms on 7th October. It was The King's Arms that sold Mevagissey to us and it didn't take long to feel very at home in this incredible village.

Living and working in a pub is an excellent way of getting to meet local characters. It is here we met the infamous fisherman, Malcolm Saunders. Malcolm was so welcoming when we moved here. We have learnt so much through him. From the months April to October, we serve up the lobsters caught by Malcolm. Occasionally Kris can also be seen on the *Morgelyn* hauling the pots.

It is only the two of us running this pub, bakery and wine shop. Kris works alone in the kitchen/bakery, making, shaping and baking for Meva Bakery which began operating in 2015. He then cooks in the evenings, serving food sourced from the boats and farms. Everything here is made by hand; the menu changes daily according to what is available on the day. The produce we are able to get is so fresh and it is an honour to be able to work with the boats from Mevagissey. We are so happy we landed here. Our focus is on sustainability and being here makes that all possible.

LEWIS FOSTER RIP

FISHERMAN

As his family it's something we will always hold true that there actually are no words that will fully describe this man! Fishing gave him a whole new family and a community which we are forever grateful for.

The Fishermen's Mission helped us no end when we all had to realise that sometimes this world is too much for some. Thank you Mevagissey for making our brother your own and making a place his daughter can always call home.

Keep hauling Lew.

JOHN 'CHUNKY' HUNKIN

SKIPPER OF CELTIC DAWN

"You have to ask permission to go fishing nowadays, and wait for them to say yes! Not like my grandfather when he came back from the War and he could fish where he wanted"

I love Mevagissey and over the years worked hard and partied hard here. There are a lot of young men come into fishing and some do well and others not so good, like any trade really. But I have three crewmen, and couldn't be without the young crew to manage the computer on board. There are so many imaginary lines in the sea now, with restrictions on what boat you have, as to where you can fish. The crew can come and go – some want just winter work and some just summer work. My two boys are both fishermen. Dan my son's been on the crew since he left school with me, and Matthew has his boat. Our family history goes back 14 generations of fishermen in Mevagissey, my father and his father.

I used to dream about fishing all day long at school, bit different when you reach 50! I worked for Freddie Turner on his boat back then; we fished all around Ireland. When it's good, it's good, and when it's bad, it's really bad. When I was younger, I was the only one enjoying the bad weather, and would be the only one out fishing; not now.

KATHERINE HUNKIN

HEADTEACHER & WIFE OF A FISHERMAN

I moved to Cornwall to take up the post of Headteacher at Mevagissey School starting in January 2008. It was a privilege becoming part of this amazing community: a lovely little school with a beautiful modern building with views of the sea and which upheld many Cornish traditions. During my first Feast Week I felt almost overwhelmed when the children arrived for their Flora dance, all wearing their best clothes, the boys with flower buttonholes and the girls with flowers in their hair. I was head at Mevagissey School for six years before moving to a school in Truro.

John Hunkin (Chunky) and I met in 2015 and we got married in 2019 in the field at Bodrugan Barton overlooking the whole bay. Having had little knowledge of the fishing industry prior to this, I've learned a great deal in this time. I've not been out fishing on the large boat, but we've been out several times on the small boat (more for fun than business) to catch mackerel and have been lucky to be treated to acrobatic dolphin displays.

We moved over the hill to Portmellon at the end of 2020 with our dog Bruce and we both enjoy swimming in the sea throughout the year. I have loved becoming part of the Hunkin tribe, particularly the past couple of years with (step) grandchildren being born into the family.

MATTHEW HUNKIN

SKIPPER

"I've loved being aboard a boat since I was a little kid. I had a punt in the garden; Mum would pack my crib and I'd go off down the garden in my smock. I spent hours throwing the nets out of the boat and pulling them back"

My Mum told me that at pre-school they used to have a big table with colourful cotton reels and shoe laces to thread. Apparently I took loads of the shoelaces, sat under the table and tied all of the chair legs together. So when someone went to push their chair away from the table they couldn't move and they were all jolting each other and crying. I was always playing with rope, practising my knots. I was often late to school; the teachers would say, "Catch any fish this morning Matthew?"

My first trip to sea was with my Dad and Ginge on the *Heather Anne* when I was 14 years old; we went to the Channel Islands. I often used my Dad's small boat until I finished school, and then I bought my first boat which I worked when I wasn't on trips at sea working with my Dad.

Ian Thomas (Ginge) sadly passed away on the 20th December 2011. Ginge was a great man and fisherman, who taught me a lot. "Keep smiling, you'll miss me when I'm gone" Ginge would say. He was right!

I now work for myself and own a fleet of three fishing vessels and you will still see me now in my smock tying knots. Fishing isn't a job; it's my way of life. The wife always jokes and says that there are more than just us in this relationship; it's the boats too! I enjoy spending my rare days off with my wife Lauren, our son Caleb and our dog.

LAUREN HUNKIN

WIFE OF A FISHERMAN

"Fishing is not a job; it's a way of life that affects us all as a family"

As wife to skipper Matthew Hunkin, we realise that the passion for fishing runs through both of us. I'm the daughter of fisherman Mike Brokenshire, and you would think that I'd be used to the silly working pattern. Everything depends on the weather and tide.

I've had a passion for fishing and the sea from a very young age, I have all my 'tickets to go to sea' and been to sea a lot with my dad. Before having our son, Matt and I would spend weekends and evenings mackerel fishing or hauling our lobster pots; the sunrises are always beautiful at sea.

Matt is at sea sometimes just for the day but at other times seven- to ten-day trips away. I'm home looking after our son Caleb, and our dog Bruno. I also deal with the mountains of paperwork that come with owning a fleet of boats. Once Matt returns from a trip, it's not time off; the boat and gear has to be maintained and got ready for the next trip. Time together as a family is cherished.

I am involved in keeping the 'Golden Maggot' diary for the committee, and helping with the Christmas Eve award of the 'Golden Maggot' to a fisherman.

Plus any free time, I help raise money for the Fishermen's Mission charity, and ensure individuals of our fishing community get help when needed.

MIKE BROKENSHIRE

FISHERMAN

"I'm very lucky to have a job I enjoy doing and to make a living out of it"

Mike came from a family of farmers and was the first member to become a fisherman. Originally from Charlestown, as a teenager he was going out fishing on small boats. When he went on to purchase his own boat, it was too big to keep in the small harbour at Charlestown, so he moved to Mevagissey harbour, which is more sheltered and safer from the often inclement weather.

"Mevagissey has a good fishing community and is one of the few places where there are up-and-coming young fishermen, it is a close-knit social group."

He enjoys the fact that the fishermen have the opportunity to meet in the coffee places on the harbour and also get together in the Social Club, a great social hub. "I have fished single-handed for most of my working life but now I have a crew, and I have taken on a young crewman."

Mike hopes that he will gain as much pleasure out of the job which he describes as "a way of life" as indeed he has during his fishing career.

DAVE HUNKIN

CHARTERED BOAT OWNER – BESSIE VEE

"Last year an angler caught my ear! That made me twitch a little bit, especially as they came towards me with a pair of pliers to cut off the barb to pull it out! They tried to make me the biggest catch of the day"

This is my 15th season running trips for anglers. It's taken years to build it up. I had gone commercial fishing for ten years before. I worked for my father for a while and then I had my own boat *Silvery Sea*. But then I went into chartered fishing. Some anglers I book used to go out with my grandad and my father before me. I get the bait and stock the boat up for every trip. I used to catch my own bait, but buy it now because there's not much mackerel out there to catch for bait myself.

The customers come from all over the country as far as Scotland and a couple guys from Holland regularly; they come from all over. They want to catch something they can't catch in their area. The season starts in April through until Christmas, depends on the weather really and the commercial fishing around the wrecks. I know what I am going to earn before I go out of the harbour. You don't have to worry about what you catch or the percentage you are going to earn and go home every evening.

LES HUNKIN

SKIPPER

"Me and my brother were put ashore to learn a living, because fishing has always been 'boom or bust'. For years we survived on pilchards till they became scarce"

The family has over 500 years of fishing history in Mevagissey. My first boat was my favourite and was called *Little Nell* which I renamed *Call of the West* after the Wurzels' song. They wrote the song 'Harbour Lights' while out on my dad's boat. They would always stay in Mevagissey if they were performing in the area. I am good friends with Peter Budd.

Morning Star was the boat I had that sank. It was full of fish and the exhaust broke and we took on water fast and I put out a mayday call. My wife heard it on the VHF radio, saying the Navy had picked up two crewmen and she didn't know if her son, husband or crewman (Zippy) were lost. But the Navy don't count skippers, only crewmen, because they go down with the ship! We were taken to RN Culdrose and put in warm baths to bring up our body temperature, and the wife brought our dry clothes but forgot our shoes; we went home in our socks!

The *Little One* was the best boat I ever had and Mrs Thatcher paid me to chop it up. The Scouts wanted the boat, but it wasn't allowed, so we broke her up on the beach besides John Moor's (boat builder). Made from Burma teak, a millionaire had her built as a pleasure boat and she was configured in Falmouth for fishing. It was a beautiful fishing boat.

When we were fishing from Newlyn, there was a storm so bad, we went down to check the boats in the harbour. We arrived and they were calling for men to go out on the boats to look for survivors from the Penlee lifeboat disaster (1981). They wouldn't let people from the same family go out together. My father and son had to wait on shore. Me and John Elvins and two Newlyn men were on the *Topaz*; 18-metre high waves and with all the boats and two lifeboats out searching for survivors in a long line, we never saw another boat, because the waves were like mountains. We only found a lifejacket that day in the sea.

I have a long service medal in Cliff Rescue Team (Coastguards), just something you do. We got called out to a gentleman who twisted and broke his leg on the top step of Polstreath Beach. We passed Dr Scott sitting and said, "I can't stop Doc; I am on a shout for someone who's broke his leg". He said, "Don't go too far because it's me!" He then told us how to splint his legs together and do all the proper first aid till the ambulance came and collected him. He was Chief Medical Officer for the NHS for Mr Harold Wilson's government and then Mrs Margaret Thatcher. I bought his house and still live in it now and we have remained very good friends.

I had to retire 30 years ago due to a serious back problem. The doctors said if I didn't I would be paralysed and in a wheelchair. We lifted such huge weights in my day; it had its effect on my back. But I have had a good life and been lucky.

JEAN HUNKIN

FISHERMAN'S WIFE

"Stinky fishy clothes drying by the Rayburn is what I remember. It was what it was and we just got on with it"

I used to listen in on the radio to find out what time he would be in for tea because he wasn't away for days at a time. My father was a fisherman and I grew up accepting the life and ways of fishing in Mevagissey, so it was nothing unusual to me, I just accepted it all and got on with it. There are generations of fishermen on both sides of our family; born in Mevagissey you just get used to it all. It was just what they did and you made the best of it. He (Les Hunkin) got up for work and came back as far as I was concerned. It seemed perfectly natural for my son John to go into fishing. As long as he was happy, that's all that mattered.

When I got a phone call from Newlyn harbour saying that Les and the lads had gone out on one of the boats looking for survivors from the RNLI Penlee lifeboat and John who was only nine years old then was with him, then I was worried that he had gone too; but they said, "No no he is in the café maid, he's alright". That was a moment that I felt fearful – the whole event was horrific.

SARAH HUNKIN

CERAMIC ARTIST

"The harbour was my playground from childhood where I was lost in rock pools and still today as a woman, it inspires my creativity and is a constant source of inspiration"

Sarah lives and works in Mevagissey. Her studio is just a short hop from the harbour and links her creativity with the fishing traditions, and she is very aware of feeling strongly connected with her heritage, from 15 generations of fishermen in Mevagissey. Sarah confesses that if she hadn't been so squeamish about catching fish she would have been a fisherwoman, but she hasn't the stomach for all the blood and guts. The fish are utilised in the next best way: in her art work. Her brother Chunky, who is a fisherman, caught a large lobster and Sarah made a mould from the lobster claw, with her skills in glazing, with wonderful, lustrous colours. Even her grandmother's crocheting is added to her fish designs that she includes for texture. Sarah connects her family and her heritage to all of her work, at any opportunity.

The harbour remains her playground, and she says it inspires her endlessly. Having her own studio space near the harbour, after gaining her Art degree in ceramics, then experiencing a lot of setbacks. She was amazed when the Sharksfin restaurant on Mevagissey harbour invited her to design their large light installations. Sarah's work at the Sharksfin is spectacular, consisting of such delicate multiples of sea urchins. She has subsequently undertaken further commissions for their other premises in Cornwall.

DAN HUNKIN
FISHERMAN

"It's what I was born into – like a family business and following in my Dad's footsteps and carrying on the family tradition"

I left school at 15 years of age and wanted to be a fisherman on my Dad's boat *Celtic Dawn*. I was a little 'eller then and my Dad sacked me when I was 16 years old. I worked as crew on other boats. I have always enjoyed the freedom of fishing. You work hard when on the boat and you get time off with your family too. It has its bad days but so does everything.

Now, I always want to impress my Dad and my Grandad as a fisherman: there are big boots to fill there! I hope one day to inherit my dad's boat. That is our plan. The Hunkin family have been fishermen in Mevagissey for over 500 years and I hope the line continues. As a fisherman you don't have a retirement plan; no fishing, and no money! I will work hard for my family to have clothes and food and maybe a nice holiday. I might go away to sea for a week but then I have a week off and I can spend that time with my family and have quality time with them. It's better than most jobs.

HEATHER COCKS

MOTHER OF FISHERMEN MATTHEW & DANIEL HUNKIN

"I never knew if I wanted my sons to go fishing at all because it's such a scary business. It felt like every Christmas there was someone lost at sea! But by default, Matt just always wanted to be a fisherman; always playing with ropes! At three years old we made him a boat in the garden with old nets, rope, fishing smock and wellies and he'd take a packed lunch and stay there all day. Dan didn't intend to be a fisherman but was swept along with fishing, it's all he knew"

Matt got a real punt at 11 yrs old and would put nets out behind the quay head after school and started his own fishing account and saved all his money to buy nets. He knew then what his dream would be and at the age of 15 he bought a boat and that is how he started.

Dan however seemed to get swept along with fishing, because an apprenticeship was a long time earning little money. Fishing he knew everyone and it was good money; but he soon discovered he was never away from the boats.

But I will never forget how at the last minute Dan had decided to help Matt on his boat when the *Heather Anne* went down – it was the first time he had said, "I'll help Matt clear the fish on the deck." Getting the call from your son to say the *Heather Anne* has gone down and not knowing if his Dad had drowned or Ginge (Ian Thomas RIP)! We all felt sick at the thought; and nothing we could do. I just felt so grateful Dan wasn't on there too. A great friend had been lost, who lived for going to sea.

Once Dan fell overboard but luckily got caught by a hook and was hanging there; if it hadn't been for the hook, Dan would have gone down with the nets! No one had noticed! His dad (John Hunkin) came home once; "I think I've hurt my finger" took off his glove and his finger fell out! Luckily his hand was so icy cold they were able to sew it back on again! They live and breathe for the job.

ROY CUNDALL RIP

FISHERMAN & LANDLORD

"My Dad was a submariner in the Royal Navy and even when they surfaced he would fish off the top with his rod and line. We have photos of him fishing off the top"

Roy was in the Navy as an electrical engineer on the submarines and when he left he would repair the electrical equipment on the fishing boats. Then he started fishing with Bernie Thomas from Mevagissey and eventually fished from Fowey and loved every minute of his fishing life with the fishing folk of Mevagissey. It was hard work to make a living from it then, despite it being a true passion. He bought and named his boat the *Gratuity* because it was literally bought with his Navy gratuity pay, and he'd go out fishing daily. The reality was that if his nets were wrecked he couldn't go fishing until they were repaired and having a family, he just simply couldn't make ends meet fishing.

Next he became landlord of the Ship Inn for six years and was always happy to have the fishermen in the pub, smelly or not – they were all welcomed. The family then moved to Fowey where Roy was landlord of The Galleon for ten years; whilst always taking the greatest interest in his grandsons' Matt and Dan Hunkin's fishing careers. He saw them doing what his dream was of being a fisherman and was so very proud of them. He often would buy them pieces of equipment, because he just loved helping the boys out.

Written by Roy's daughter, Heather Cocks

BRITANNIA

FREDDIE TURNER RIP

SKIPPER & FISHING LEGEND

"He fished from many ports but Mevagissey was his home port and the place he loved to be"

Freddie Turner was born in Portloe into a fishing family; he started at an early age fishing from Portloe with his grandfather, mainly fishing for crab and lobster. On leaving school he was boatbuilding with his brother for a short time, building *Britannia II* for him and his Dad to work off the beach at Portloe. Around this time he went to Mevagissey, working during the winter months with Graham and Melville Mills on the *Snowdrop*. Graham and Freddie became great buddies. During the summertime he worked *Britannia II*, crabbing between the ports of Mevagissey and Portloe.

In 1974 Freddie moved to Mevagissey to live and in 1975 Freddie with his brother John had a 30-foot boat built at G.P. Mitchell and Sons for crabbing, inshore and further afield in the Channel. This boat was now based at Mevagissey. He was always looking to improve his ability to fish and in 1978 during many trips to Scotland to purchase a larger vessel, he bought the 40-foot boat from Peterhead called *The Wanderer* with the intention of longlining and fishing for crab and lobster in the Channel. It was found this vessel was not suitable, so he sold it back to Scotland.

His next boat was 35-foot *Britannia IV* built by John Moor at Charlestown. By the time *Britannia IV* was launched the type of fishery Freddie wanted to pursue had altered to gill nets and tangle nets. He was always trying different types of netting and was one of the pioneers of successful wreck net fishing. In 1986 *Britannia V*, a 50-foot boat, was launched in Scotland, built by Alexander Noble and Sons of Girvan. He worked this boat with his loyal crew of five, one being Ian Thomas (Ginge) who sadly drowned in a fishing boat accident in 2011. He joined *The Wanderer* in 1978.

Freddie made *Britannia V* a very successful fishing boat working in all weathers, not just around the South West but also tuna fishing in the Bay of Biscay and beyond, also to the north west of Scotland working west of the Shetlands and Western Isles for cod and monkfish.

He was taken ill whilst fishing in Scotland and sadly died in May 1998 at the age of 45 years.

He was highly respected throughout the fishing industry and his name often crops up in conversation within the fishing communities today.

JOHN LEACH

RING NET MAKER

I came ashore from fishing in 1983; 'cos we sold commercial fishing gear and our business was known as Leach & Turner. I sold that business in 2002 to a company in Newlyn and intended to work there for 12 months and stayed six years!

I specialise in ring nets and there's a boat in Mevagissey I supply to called the *Galwad-Y-Mor:* she's the only ring netter from Mevagissey. It's owned by Chris Blamey; it's a real fishing speciality. All the other ring netter boats that I look after are at Newlyn.

Once the ring net has been shot around the shoal of fish, you then got to keep the boat from drifting into the net. So you have a smaller boat beside it with a rope to keep it pulled out away from the net. Whereas the boats at Newlyn don't do that; they are built for it and have what they call 'side thrusters' to push the boat sideways out of the net. The nets are manufactured in Denmark.

Gill net fishing started in late 70s and I started dealing with Denmark in 1984 and that's where my connection started. All nets to do with the fishing today comes from abroad. There are no net manufacturers at all in the UK now, Denmark, Portugal, China, Japan, and Thailand; it all takes a long time to get these things. Over the years companies have died out for different reasons in the UK.

SID ALLEN

LOCAL HISTORIAN & EX-FISHERMAN

"There were a couple weeks of easterlies going up over the lighthouse, but once you got through and up inside the Black Head, it wasn't too bad. Coming back in wasn't so nice!"

I'm 10th-generation Charlestown, but most of my fishing life was from Mevagissey. I started in the boatyard with John Moor in Charlestown and then he moved to Mevagissey. It started me fishing for a year with Mike Avent. I then went back to Charlestown crabbing until I got a call from Bryan Zippy; would I do a trip with Lawrence Letcher, on the *Julante*?

I then formed a partnership with Mike Brokenshire over the years; I'd lay my boat up October time and work with Mike (1995) until I retired in 2018. We would start the handlining up around the Eddystone. As that fish went east, we would then fish down Mounts Bay up until Christmas handlining for mackerel. Then we would work 100 cod nets; that's a lot of gear! That's as much as a six-handed Newlyn boat would work; me and Mike would work that up Fowey with six long strings and they were long old days. One winter we never missed a day for 46 days!

I worked 300 lobster pots on my own in the summer months at Charlestown but Mevagissey was always close to my heart. I used to look forward to going down there and then February, I'd be looking forward to Charlestown again!

PAUL LAWSON

FISHERMAN

I worked on the *Celtic Dawn* with John Hunkin, and his son Matt Hunkin trained me when I started. I've got a few little tales I could tell but they wouldn't be printable for the book! What I loved about the job more than anything was it was like being a family; just like my Army and fire service days. You live and breathe together; everybody had each other's back. It was fantastic. Sometimes in rough seas it was a case of grabbing you by the scruff of your neck and stopping you going over. Those boys made me unbelievably welcome.

In the winter months we'd go wrecking and Joe Chesterfield used to come with us. I used to start singing a song and Joe would start singing too. I'd call out, "Joe you got earworm again?" And he'd deny he had. I'd start another song and sure enough he'd sing it. Every string we'd pull on, I would sing a different song and he'd shout, "You've got me again!" The crew would shake their heads and laugh.

I was on the boat for three years with those boys and I was sick every day at sea! I just loved being with the lads and going to sea. They said I put bait out for the fish! I had three operations on my left hand due to Dupuytren's contracture (the Viking disease) but now I can't clasp with my hand. I can't hold a rope or eat my dinner properly, otherwise I'd still be fishing now. I absolutely loved it and miss it every day.

JAMES WILLIAMS

SKIPPER

"I was working with a bloke in Lulworth Cove who'd worked in Mevagissey in the 70s and said, 'If you want to go fishing Mevagissey is the place to do it.' I saw a job advertised with Mike West online, packed the car up and moved here. That was 15 years ago"

I grew up in a place called Lulworth Cove in Dorset and fished out of there for a number of years. I've always worked on boats since school; even ran boat trips out of Lulworth Cove in the summer months and then would fish during the winter months, weather permitting.

I run the *Gina C* boat for Matthew Hunkin now. For about three years I've had two of my own boats, called the *Lioness* and the *Magnum*. Someone else ran that one for me in Mevagissey but I've sold them both now. I prefer working for someone else; it takes the stress out of the job for me. There's a lot of responsibility in fishing. Life is getting more complicated and you need to adjust to the changes. We land the fish at Plymouth and moor up in Mevagissey in the winter and land and keep it in Brixham for the summer.

JONNIE COLLINGS

SKIPPER OF THE BUCCANEER

"It's not a job. It's a way of life. Everything you do is for fishing. It's been a real hard winter with the storms"

I've been fishing since I was a kid, on a 'little crabber' with Frank Trevarton and then worked with Michael Barron for eight years. Eventually I got my own boat in '94 the *Buccaneer*, working all-year-round from hand lines to nets, catching all that is available from squid, mackerel, bass, whiting, spider crabs and anything within our quota. I love it for the freedom, when the weather allows us. It's not easy for the youngsters here, waiting on the good weather to fish and earn a living.

We were fishing off Porthscatho and the wind freshened easterly, headed for home and said, "This is weather you'd lose your raft!" As we came around Chapel Point, she rolled away and I heard a bang and there was my raft off the roof, in the water! We came around to pick the raft up, and its ropes got tied around the props. Thought we'd lose her that day on the rocks! But luckily Matt Cave came up around and towed us into harbour.

My boat was in the film 'Bait' that just won a BAFTA award and I was invited down for its first showing in Newlyn to watch it, with the production team and actors and all involved. The *Buccaneer* and number are visible in the film, so the public ask if it was the boat used in the film.

BRADLEY COLLINGS

FISHERMAN

I fished before I left school with dad Jonathon. It's all I've done. I've been full-time for the last eight years. Work alongside Andy Shaw on the *Defiant* and we're mainly trawling and twin rigging. We all fish hard and play harder!

The recent fuel prices have just doubled. It was 60p a litre and now £1.38. It makes a big difference; we're earning far less. Well, you can't moan about it - I'm sure it'll come round.

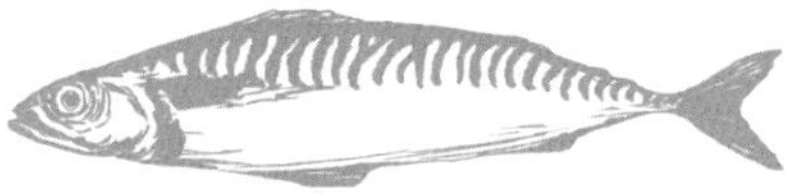

IAN 'GINGE' THOMAS RIP

FISHERMAN

As a family we will forever be grateful to the Fishermen's Mission for the support given to us in the days, weeks and months following Ginge's death. These visits were a great comfort to our Mum and even years later, if one of the Mission's officers were in the village, they'd pop up to see Mum and stay for a cuppa – little things like this mean so much.

Sian, Ali & Denise

(Ginge's sisters)

LISA HIGMAN

LANDLADY, HARBOUR TAVERN

"Mevagissey is a small, tight community and the fishermen are the very heart of the community. It's really special because of the fishing industry that is here!"

I have been a landlady here for twelve years. My grandad always visited here on a Wednesday for his fish and chips and his free beers; a very traditional man, he played in the brass band and knew a lot of the fishermen through the years. The fishermen always showed him such respect and that's why they are special people to know. I think the job makes them special people; being out on the water, coping with so much, it makes them so real, as people.

I've been strict with the fishermen and probably thrown most of them out at one time or another; but I have deep respect for them all. When they go out to sea in the weather and conditions and catch sometimes nothing! It's hard. It's like my business, I might sell one beer or have a really busy night; you just never know what to expect. The same as the fishing boats; they might have a great catch or really bad, they still have fuel to buy, pay the crew and expenses and you can see the pressure is really hard for them. It's their livelihood, and all are self-employed.

I will never forget 'Ginge' (Ian Thomas fisherman RIP 2011), because from when I started here, he took me under his wing. Not only was I a woman, and from St Austell; I was gay! He defended my corner, he was here every day for ten months when he had a knee operation and became the closest thing I could have of a husband. We bonded and shared everything together and I loved him, as did my family. He was a genuine and good man. The grief felt by us all was massive and the harbour was packed as his hearse came through the quayside.

We've had so many wedding receptions, parties, anniversaries here of the fishermen, all of them very special days, that felt magical.

JACKIE CHARLES AND SELINA CROWSON

THE CELLAR BAR

"We went out on a fishing boat out of Mevagissey one year to see the Red Arrows. It was a flat calm sea and still we were moving about; it was hard to stand up. I don't know how the fishermen do it – it's the hardest job in the world. We see them in the bar. They work hard and play hard too."

Friends for 30 years, Jackie met Selina before she owned the Cellar Bar. Selina remembers her 21st birthday. Selina had failed her driving test and had been made redundant the same day. That night Selina was supposed to go to her party but she stayed in the pub with Jackie and got drunk. Jackie said she'd get her a job at the bar, she'd be fine. She got a job and worked the next day at the Cellar Bar, albeit hungover.

Jackie purchased the Cellar Bar in her late 20s. Her friend Selina worked with her at the start and then came back some years later. Selina thought Jackie was joking when she said she was going to buy the bar: "It was a big risk but it has worked. It was made for her, she's a brilliant landlady."

MOLLY MOORE

"Mevagissey is a lovely place to live and a nice place to bring up children"

Molly lives in a cottage in Cliff Street. On a bleak winter's morning when I visited, the welcoming fire was roaring and the cosy warmth of what has been her home for over 72 years helped me to understand why she has lived there for so long. At 95, she is very sprightly and walks down to the village daily to do her shopping, check on Billy in The Fountain and meet for coffee with friends.

Molly grew up in Par near to the harbour and docks. She talked fondly of her childhood playing with the children on the Dutch boats which were used to transport the china clay to places such as France. Living next to the gas works also had its advantages as she and her friends would take potatoes down to where they pulled the coke out and bake them! She also remembers when oil cake was brought in to the warehouse on the docks where the farmers would come and buy it to feed the cattle. There were always many cats there and she loved playing with them, obviously where her love of cats stems from! Her handsome ginger cat Willow was often seen patrolling the harbour, admired by visitors and locals alike.

"Living next to the water, I loved boats and my grandfather, a retired sea captain, had a 14-foot rowing boat built for me when I was 14 years old. I used to row in the regattas in Par. When I moved to Mevagissey, it came with me and eventually became Billy's first boat.

I met my husband, William Richard Moore at a football match at St Blazey. When we married, we lived with his mother in Mevagissey but moved to Cliff Street when Billy was born.

I worked all my married life, for 17 years I was in the Ship Inn and later moved to the King's Arms. Soon after Billy took over The Fountain I went to work there. On Saturday mornings I would make 30 or so pasties which he would sell at the bar.

My husband worked on the quay in the fishing stores and then after a brief time in the building trade, took on his own fishing round which was very successful. He would buy the fish from the Mevagissey fisheries and sell it in and around St Austell and even as far as Newquay. He did this till he was 70 and then for three years until he retired completely, worked on the quay in a fishing shop owned by Sue Lakeman."

Molly is fiercely independent and loves cooking. Every Sunday she cooks a roast dinner for her neighbour. They take it in turns to buy the meat. In return he checks on Molly, ensures that her coal and wood is brought in and is there to help her if needed. A true reflection of Meva community spirit.

William and Laura Moore

WILLIAM MOORE

MOORE'S GREENGROCERS

I come from a family of Williams: my grandfather was William Richard, my dad William Earnest, myself William Richard and now my first born, Wilfred! As a child I spent a lot of time with my grandad. He had a fish round and I remember him and my nan preparing the crab on the kitchen table and him filleting fish outside the house in the back of the van. I used to join him on his fish rounds, often getting a few buns as treats from the old ladies! Grandad ran the fish hut on the quay 'til he was 72 and I used to help out in the summer, selling wet fish, cockles and mussels. In my teens I used to fish with my friends out quay for mackerel, often until dark. Fishing was a hobby but I never wanted to become a fisherman. I went to Plymouth University and studied microbiology. It was great; I could study and watch my football team Plymouth Argyle!

When I left university, I worked on building sites and continued to do so until 2012 when I fell from some scaffolding and badly injured my back. It was after that when Laura and I decided to buy the greengrocer's in the village. I've known many of the locals, our customers, since I was a kid. It's a great job.

Since then, we have had our two sons, Wilfred born in 2016 and Ralph in 2019. It doesn't feel like work, it's just like playing shop like we used to do at school!

BILLY MOORE

LANDLORD, THE FOUNTAIN INN

"I have probably seen Meva change over the years more than anyone will ever see again"

Bill was born in 1947, the only son of Molly and William Moore. His memories are of a very different Mevagissey from what it is today. On the quayside he remembers there being three coal merchants and three fish merchants which over the years have been replaced by flats, shops and cafes.

"In the mid-sixties we were lucky, we had lots of fish quays, boats and fish factories operating. Then came commercialisation and it all changed.

I had my first boat when I was six; a punt given to me by my mother. She was a champion rower and the boat had been built for her and she taught me to row. I used to take the boat out on my own. I couldn't swim and didn't wear a lifejacket. As kids we used to go down to Polstreath Beach, take a packed lunch and stay there all day, only coming home when we were hungry. If we weren't at the beach we would be playing down in the woods. We had a great time; it was a very different life to what children have nowadays.

I went out on my first longline fishing trip at ten years old with Graham and Melville Mills on their boat, the *Snowdrop*. I used to stand with a big dip net and as the fish fell out it was my job to scoop them up and put them in a maund (basket) and I was paid according to the quantity. However, when the ship was in the harbour I was given all the mucky jobs to do: clean out the bilges, the cuddy, wheelhouse and scrub the deck. Lots of kids did the same but it wouldn't be allowed nowadays.

I went to grammar school which I didn't really enjoy and on a Friday evening in November 1964, I came home and told Mother I was going to Plymouth School of Navigation for an interview to go in the Merchant Navy. I started in January 1965 and after twelve months of training I passed out and went to London to sign up to a company called Holder Brothers. I joined my first ship on January 3rd 1966. I became disillusioned with the Merchant Navy and returned to Mevagissey."

Bill had a yearning to go to South Africa but life was to take a very different pathway. After leaving the navy he needed to get a job.

"Melville asked me if I could go and help him on a couple of fishing trips and 14 years later, I was still fishing. It was in the heyday when mackerel fishing was good in the winter."

It was during this time that Bill married Mary and had a son, William. They lived in a cottage in Cliff Street. However, fishing became poor and it was hard to make ends meet. The tenancy of The Fountain Inn came up in 1981, and although many people applied, Mary and Bill were successful.

"I said I'd do it for a maximum of ten years, but I have now been here for 41! It's been hard work but great fun. I've met many people and had heartbreak along the way but it's been good."

Matthew Mills with his Mum, Pauline

WILLIAM 'MELVILLE' MILLS RIP

SKIPPER OF THE SNOWDROP

My father and his two-year elder brother Graham were born and raised in Polkirt Hill, Mevagissey. Their house, facing East Wharf, had views of Mevagissey Bay and the Gribben and fishing was in their blood from a young age. Their love for fishing was vehemently discouraged by their mother Julie, who was worried about the dangers of this perilous livelihood.

The brothers learnt their trade on the *Investor* in the 1950s, under Jim Behenna and then went on to fish on the *Snowdrop*, which they subsequently jointly bought. The *Snowdrop*, a 45-foot, 1926-built Cornish lugger stood out in emerald green with black trim and a cream and brown wheelhouse. They fished predominantly for pilchards and mackerel and longlined for turbot, conger and ling in the summer. Crewman Billy Moore recalls hauling up 365 turbot on one shoot; "one for every day of the year!" This equated to circa 243 stone in weight. Some characters that crewed on the *Snowdrop* included: Jonathan Mills (Graham's son), Billy Moore, Alan 'Bonzo' Littlejohns, Billy Warren, Edgar Hocking and Jim Mills. My father, Graham and the crew were devastated when they learnt at sea of the death of a beloved crew member Andrew Warren, taken from life in his youth in a fatal car crash.

In 1979, the brothers went their separate ways in fishing. Graham bought the *Blejaneyhre* and Dad took on a tosher named the *Renee*; often accompanied by Billy Warren or Jamie Elvins. He would fish south-east Cornwall again but would take tourists out on day trips in the summer as this provided a steady income when the fishing industry was in decline. The decline in fishing during the 70s and 80s was the reason my dad never encouraged me to fish, hence me joining the RAF in 1988. Dad retired from fishing in the late 80s due to chronic back pain but was never happier doing anything else than fishing. When people asked him about how he was doing in retirement, he always replied, "The best thing about retirement was thinking about retirement." This for me underlined where he was most happy, aside from his beloved family that is – fishing!

Written by Melville's son, Matthew Mills

COLIN HAM

NET RIGGER

"I did go ashore to work for three years but the sea drew me back again. You can't get it out of your system"

I came to Mevagissey fishing in 1982 for a bloke called Charlie Saunders on the *Scathross* and had about eight years with Charlie, then I bought my own little boat and went on me own. I've been in and out of boats all of my life really. I've owned a fair few boats over the years in the harbour, had a little boat called the *Girl Amanda*, then the *Marlin Gee*, the *Diligent*. I worked for Peter Blamey on the *Girl Rachel* and the *Galwad-Y-Mor*, *Celtic Dawn*, the *Little One'*... I could be here till 10 o'clock tonight naming boats.

I started stitching nets when I was 16 years old and then started again for Peter Blamey. There wasn't enough to keep me going but because Matt Hunkin has two boats, I basically stitch nets six days a week for Matt. I'm getting older now and at 62, going to sea every day, it does take it out of you! But I still go back out to sea. Went with James Williams about six weeks ago for a week up to Weymouth. I did love it but it's taken until now to get over it! But that's about it now. I stitch nets in a barn near Caerhays, and drive there every day with my Jack Russell, Dave.

CHARLIE SAUNDERS

RETIRED FISHERMAN & SKIPPER

"I did fishing all my life; nothing else for 40 years and no regrets at all. I brought up my family, paid my mortgage off; anyone that was keen always made a living out of it"

I always wanted to do fishing and my family were all seafarers for generations really, but into schooners and trading vessels rather than fishing, going around the world, but for my father who was a teacher at Camborne Technical College. I left Camborne Tech' at 17 and took up fishing and now retired from it. I started off with Jim Elvins and worked for him 12 months, then worked for Rodney Ingram for about 18 months and then I went off on my first boat the *Susan Jane*; bought it off Andrew Lakeman.

I had a number of boats until my final boat I had built about 34 years ago called the *Red Vixen*. It was built in Looe and now in Lymington with her new owner. Now I go down on the quay, because you miss the people you know, but I don't go out to sea no more.

PAULA SAUNDERS

MEVA GIRL & WIFE OF RETIRED FISHERMAN CHARLIE SAUNDERS

"I have great memories of singing along to Bohemian Rhapsody making mackerel boxes on the quay"

I married Charlie 42 years ago. Like my father, he was a fisherman. When I had James, our son, I remember the midwife coming in and saying not to worry about Charlie coming to visit me smelling of fish, as James would have to get used to it! Of course James is now a fisherman!

When I was 12 I used to work in Kelly's on the quay. I remember one day being given the job of making the doughnuts. I still think that was the best job in the world! During the 70s, when there was a bumper catch of mackerel, my friends, including Ali Thomas and I used to go down to the Co-op and make mackerel boxes for hours on end. At that time, Queen's Bohemian Rhapsody was in the charts, we would spend week after week listening to it, singing along. We produced hundreds of boxes, it was fun!

I have had so many different jobs including working with Mum in the B&B for twenty years; worked in an estate agents; various cafés and now as well as working part-time in the Aquarium I am a carer and support worker.

JAMES SAUNDERS

SKIPPER

"I was earning so well from catching pilchards as a teenager, that I had saved and bought my own boat, the *Maria Q*, by the time I was 18 years old"

I started off fishing when I was 12 years old with a punt, and worked a few nets in the bay catching pilchards with my cousin, and we did really well up until I was about 16 years old. My dad then retired and I took over the *Red Vixen* and worked down Falmouth Bay and gradually went further afield for turbot; then on to wrecks to catch pollock.

Last year I decided not to work away so much and take on a smaller boat and work on my own, and don't have the problem of finding a crew. I can rely on myself to do the job that way. I have had to spend almost a year investing and getting the boat ready, plus get a set of nets together. But it's been a long wet winter with not much fishing. But I just wouldn't do any other job, fishing is my life. I thought as a kid of either being in the Army or going fishing, but as my dad had a boat, I naturally went with fishing.

Fishing: you never know when you will get a good catch, or earn a good wage, it's something you can't predict. It's very much hit and miss. One week it can be great and then the bad weather comes in and you don't earn anything. Then there is the safety factor too but I've always been lucky and never got hurt or injured. The young lads coming into fishing have a lot to learn about safety in all weathers and conditions. Working on my own now, I always wear my lifejacket and with the new ones we have been given that have personal locators on them, if I went over the side, they would locate me in the sea and pick me up. You don't even know you have the new lifejackets on and they protect your neck from the sun. They've done a good job designing them for fishermen.

SOPHIE WEST

WIFE OF LEE WEST

"Lee's first love is his boat. Even going to sea when I was overdue with our first child and having to phone him at 5am to say I think you better come home! All was well and he made it in time for the birth of our daughter"

When Lee is in from sea most of the time there's work to be done on the gear or the boat. So a whole day off as a family is very special. We're lucky enough to live in the village so when Lee is working down the harbour, we're able to walk down to see him, hard at work; or leaning on someone's truck having a chat!

Lee's fishing can range from a whole day's trip from Mevagissey or two or three days to a couple of weeks. The smell after a long trip away can be quite something. But as the boys say, it's the smell of money and nothing a good boiled wash and good shower can't fix!

Long spell of bad weather can take its toll and be stressful. Fishermen want to be at sea as many days of the year as possible and don't like to be stuck in for bad weather. No fishing equals no money. On the other hand if I had a quid for every time I heard, "Should be at sea today" we'd be millionaires!

LEE WEST

FISHERMAN & SKIPPER

"I'm the well behaved one... and I'm well known for my appetite"

The skipper of the *Copious*, I've been a full-time fisherman since leaving school 14 years ago. Fishing after school before that, from age of 12; I bought my first proper boat at 14. The day I left school, travelled up with father from Mevagissey to collect a boat in Scotland. We've fished in Wales. We'd be away for a couple of weeks and then travel back home for a few days. Fished all over really in and around Brixham, Newlyn, France, Shoreham, Isle of Man mainly scalloping and when we're trawling we'd catch cuttlefish, haddock, whiting, squid etc.

I'm married to Sophie and we had our first baby in June. Sophie would probably say of me when I'm home and in the morning, open the curtains and it doesn't look windy, "Should have gone fishing really!"

We've done a lot of rowing in the past. I'm part of the local gig team; one year we managed to get a fishermen's crew together when we were at the World Pilot Gig Championships on the Isles of Scilly. It was good, we were all at home at the same time. We're quite friendly with many of the gig rowers, we know many, especially those from Newquay and Cadgwith.

JACK WEST

FISHERMAN & SKIPPER

"I feel I can hold my head high and say we are the next generation of fishermen, doing our bit for the fishing industry of Mevagissey"

The good part of being your own boss is you can choose when and where you want to go fishing. Obviously the good parts are when the weather is good and bad parts are when you can't get out for weeks. I have been a skipper for nearly three years with an under-ten metre trawler, called *Ann Louise*. We are quite restricted by where we can go and what we can do, but on the whole we are lucky being a smaller boat, we can fish in places others can't.

I worked as a crew member after leaving college to do gamekeeping, but fishing was in my blood and it just pulled me back and I worked with my dad fishing and other crews for five years. I skippered for two years on the boat *Equinox*. If you are willing to work hard it's a good wage, but there are times when there is nothing and it's a struggle. So you have to be prepared for the good and bad times. Hence if you have a 'good catch' you're reluctant to tell others where it's to. It makes it fun and gives us some competition. But we are always supportive with our fellow fishermen if anything goes wrong; you help them out.

My dad manages the paperwork side of fishing. It helps so much that we don't have that worry while we concentrate on the fishing, weather and care of the boat; it's a great combination. It's very much a family affair.

NICK WEST

FISHERMAN

We've two family boats, *Copious* and *Ann Louise*. Jack the youngest is the skipper of *Ann Louise* and Lee my eldest son is the skipper of *Copious*. A fisherman since 1979; brother, uncle and cousin are fishermen, Dad was in the merchant navy. Mother's side of the family were from Grimsby and the father's side from Essex, all seafarers. I've lived here since I was three. We don't think the move was fishing-related; the fishing industry was in a state then. Grandad was a marine engineer and he retired here and I think that's why the family joined him.

I've worked with all my family and they've worked with me. We've had some fall-outs, my brother sacked me before, I've sacked my son before... we've all worked together which was exciting, Lee straight after he finished school and Jack went to college and had a job but soon joined us. If you're born here or live here, you're dragged into the harbour life, then you're under a spell and then you don't know anything different.

We've been looking for a house with some land as Jo my wife has some animals. Obviously there's nowhere suitable in Mevagissey so it's at Polmassick, on the outskirts of Mevagissey. There was no interest in buying it because it had a vineyard attached, so we thought we'd try to keep it going. It's more of Jo and my mother-in-law who run it.

LINDSAY WEST

WIFE OF MIKE WEST

You had no idea when they would be home or how long they would be at sea for or anything. It was always really difficult with a young family. But at least now with mobile phones and modern communications you can be in constant touch, several times a day; they can get updated on what's happening. But when Mike was away a lot when the kids were younger, he missed so much about the children's growing up. It could be all the insignificant things they never knew about the children, by saying, "Oh you'd never guess what they did today!" To tell Mike days or weeks later; you just didn't do it. Sometimes he'd be away six weeks at a time; that's a long time in a child's life.

I had very strong friendships with my girl friends. Most of my friends were fishermen's wives and it was understood that when Mike was away, we could see each other often. It was understood when Mike was home, that would be my focus. That was a hard balance, but my friends respected the situation and it showed the strength of the community, because everyone is involved one way or another with fishing. And it's a real safety net around when people can see what's involved; you see the good and the bad. What rivalries or difficulties there are with you because it's all very competitive; but when the chips are down, everybody is there. There is always a common thread through the generations and mutual respect.

MIKE WEST

SKIPPER OF MEVAGISSEY FERRY & MATE ON FISHING BOATS

"We came home from the Scillies for the gig rowing championships and the whole family rowed gigs. My daughter Laura had just passed her driving test and dropped me at 6.30am at Bodmin roundabout and 20 past ten that night I was in Wick; bingo! Pint in my hand and a place to stay; ready to meet the boat in the north of Scotland"

I was at school with Colin Williams and I would go out at evenings and weekends, even when he was still part-time. I came home one day from a trip and my dad said Colin had a job for me and that was my start of fishing in Mevagissey. Colin had a company Crystal Claws and I worked for about eight years for him and skippered the *Silver Crest* that was the biggest in the harbour then. We had four crewmen on the boat and now they only work with two and a lot smaller boats that are more efficient; they do the job without a big crew. You got to make a living for however many men are on the boat.

I now drive the Mevagissey Ferry in the summer and then usually from October to March I go away on big trawlers, in the wheelhouse, sailing out of Brixham. I have two or three people I work for and still enjoy it. It allows me to do what I enjoy without relying on savings. I enjoy going around different places working; it means time away but at least when you are home, you're home.

LYNNE GOULDSMITH

WIFE OF VERNON

"I didn't know there were two 4 o'clocks in a day, until I married a Mevagissey fisherman!"

Vernon has always fished out of Meva, even when he had a full-time job working away at sea, as the captain of a dredger. So when we got together, it was important that I adapted to his way of life. You quickly get used to the odour that accompanies your loved one when they first return home from sea! Thankfully the washing machine and a good shower deal with the practicalities of that. But it is important not to tumble-dry their favourite socks, hats and thermals!

It is impossible not to worry when they are at sea, especially when the weather takes a turn for the worse, or if they are away for several days and nights. However, you have to trust that they have the skills and knowledge to keep themselves safe, and there is a great camaraderie between all the fishermen. When they are out at sea they all look out for each other and help each other out. When times are tough, and to stop me worrying, I remember the words of the song of the Breton Fisherman's Prayer:

"Protect me, O Lord, for my boat is so small and your sea is so wide"

Being a Mevagissey fisherman is difficult and dangerous, but they wouldn't want to do any other job, as fishing is in their blood. I just hope it helps them to know they are fully supported by their 'significant others' at home.

VERNON GOULDSMITH

GORRAN HAVEN & MEVAGISSEY FISHERMAN

"Fishing is a way of life to me"

Fishing allows you to do what you want, when you want – you are your own boss. You can go out on the boat, away from everything on shore.

I have a small boat, 21-footer: big enough to keep me out of trouble big, enough to keep me in trouble! I work single-handed through the spring to autumn, and in winter time I join a crew on a larger boat. I used to work in the North Sea, for 24 years – it was very cold up there. It's much warmer down here. Everyone gets on. If there is a problem, we help each other out, you can rely on each other big time. Loads will stand on the quay and watch you do something wrong and tell you how to do it right afterwards (he chuckles). But they are all a good bunch of people. They are real, genuine people.

REVEREND CANON MARION BARRETT

RECTOR OF ST PETER'S CHURCH MEVAGISSEY

"St Peter's Church has been on this site for generations"

My father was a fireman who came to Cornwall to help with the *Torrey Canyon* oil spill in 1967 and fell in love with the county. As a teenager I moved with my family to Newquay in 1970.

In 2005, following a long line of clergy who have cared for community and church, I was installed as the Rector of St Peter's in Mevagissey: a strong community with fishing and harbour at its heart. The church has been on this site for generation upon generation, from the time of early Celtic saints, St Meva and St Issey, who give their names to the parish of Mevagissey. The church was later dedicated to St Peter, the patron saint of fishermen, for fishing was the heart of the community with it being the chief centre of pilchard fishery in the 18th century. The church is full of images and items that relate to fishing in biblical stories and community life. It has been a joy to celebrate Sea Sunday during the year, with choirs, Harbour Masters and many others taking part. St Peter's hosts the children from school at various times over the year and plays a part retelling the bible stories, including stories of St Peter, at assemblies. The community and folk from far and wide come together for Meva Feast Week to celebrate, centred around St Peter's Day on 29th June.

The Church is a sacred place where community gather to mark the joyful and sorrowful times of life, receiving care, support and reassurance in times of crisis. Many a fisher family has celebrated weddings, christenings and funerals with family and community, and it has been my delight to share with them.

Thank you Mevagissey, centred around the sea, for being a wonderful community.

LARRY BEARDSMORE

CHURCHWARDEN ST PETER'S CHURCH MEVAGISSEY

"St Peter, as a former fisherman, is the patron saint of net makers, shipbuilders and fishermen"

After spending many holidays from thc 1970s scuba diving around the Cornwall coast, I finally retired here in Meva with my wife in 2007. When I joined the congregation at St Peter's, the Rev Canon Marion Barrett was already and still is the vicar. In 2016 I was elected Churchwarden, taking over from Jenny Keast and working alongside Graham Bulkeley. A previous Churchwarden Francis Hunkin was instrumental, alongside a newly-formed committee, in rejuvenating Feast Week which always includes St Peter's Day on 29th June. On the Tuesday of the week-long celebration, St Peter's organises a sports event at the school with refreshments served to the children. During the evening hymns appropriate for sailors and fishermen are sung around the village and harbour. Finally, a brass band leads the procession for the flora dance. If you go into church there are many references to the sea and fishermen: for example, the Altar window shows references to boats and the sea and the ceiling is constructed like an upturned boat. One of the Lady Chapel windows was funded by a sea captain. We also have a painting depicting Jesus entering Meva harbour. Although many fishermen do not attend Sunday services, they and their families are great supporters of the church, as can be witnessed on festival days.

"Let us at this time pray for our own fishing community adapting to massive change, for wisdom in implementing policies that will sustain and renew fishing stocks whilst ensuring the viability of fishing businesses."

SANDRA BEARDSMORE

CHAIR OF GOVERNORS AT MEVAGISSEY COMMUNITY PRIMARY SCHOOL

"As a mother, grandmother and retired teacher, I am very proud to have been Chair of Governors since 2011"

At Mevagissey School parents, staff and governors work together so that all our children have the best chance to develop to their full potential. Above all, we want the children to take pride in everything they achieve, to grow and learn with confidence. We are committed to do the best for all our children and we aim to provide a happy and safe environment, where everyone is valued. Through challenge, encouragement and support we promote the qualities of enthusiasm, curiosity, creativity, confidence and determination. Our children, many of them from fishermen's families, are at the heart of our school community. Classes are named after sea creatures: starfish, dolphins, jellyfish, seals and sea turtles. We are proud to be part of the Cornwall Education Learning Trust (CELT). We benefit from collaboration with and support from other schools in the Trust.

Our curriculum includes local visits to Polstreath beach for our 'Beach School', and classes visit our harbour, the aquarium and museum, learning about the lives of local families including fishermen.

Our children and families always enjoy taking part in Feast Week, processing around the harbour and village on Fish Sunday, dressing up to take part in the 'Flora', dancing to the recreation ground to open the Saturday fête, finally competing in the traditional Tug of War!

Mevagissey School set at the top of a hill with its stunning sea views, is a place where everyone is excited about coming to school and everyone has a genuine desire to learn!

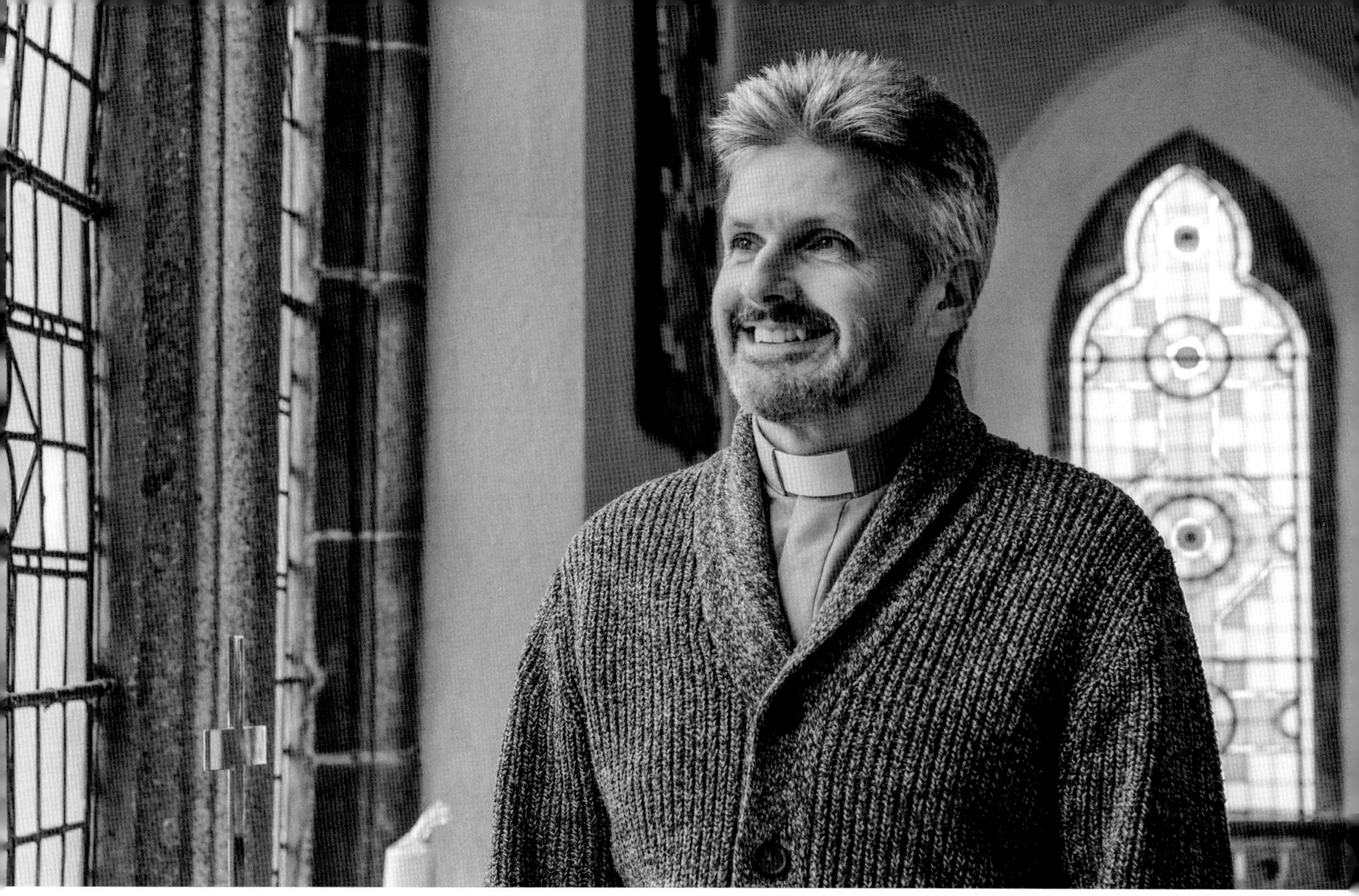

PAUL BENNEY

METHODIST MINISTER

"I am a proud Cornishman"

As of October 2021, I have the pleasure of living in the lovely village of 'Mev' and being its Methodist and URC (United Reform Church) minister – whilst having care of seven other chapels in the area! The Anglican church in Mev' is St Peter's, so when the renovations on the congregational chapel were complete, it was decided it be called St Andrew's; the two fishermen saints being brothers.

I am a proud Cornishman all the way 'up-country' from my roots near Porthleven, father to four lovely young people and blessed husband to Esther! As a minister I wear the 'dog collar' from which many run, some are intrigued and others ask the oddest questions. Many meet the collar with embarrassed indifference unless I am needed; none of which I mind. My hero had very much the same welcome and think what they did to Him! It is a privilege to walk a while with people in deep need, loss or celebration, to be the representative of the local chapel, share a laugh or tears, lots of tea and if I'm lucky – cake.

The church supports the fishing community where possible, and annually gives thanks to celebrate through our 'Harvest of the Sea' service in October.

It is fundamental that we as a village support each other through our community whether it be via clubs, social activities, sports events or the church; and being a friend to those who are in need, vulnerable or lonely. May God bless his home and ours!

SUE COATES

RETIRED HEADTEACHER AT MEVAGISSEY COMMUNITY PRIMARY SCHOOL

My first encounter with the Mevagissey fishermen was just a few weeks after moving to our beautiful village. Our eldest son had gone to the harbour to watch the waves in an easterly. We had no idea then how dangerous this was. He was swept off the steps by the lighthouse, falling down the cliff. The fishermen acted immediately; they called the ambulance and found out where we were living and put all their trucks next to him to prevent further soaking. True legends all of them!

Four years later I became Head Teacher of Mevagissey School and enjoyed 21 wonderful years there. The fishermen helped the school in countless ways and were a massive support. Every Feast Week they helped with transporting props and staging. It was very special watching youngsters from fishing families learning to scull across the harbour, then eventually becoming fishermen themselves.

When the new school opened, the old school bell was renovated and moved to the new school. Rupert Edwardes made a superb bell pull to complete the bell. It was intricately woven, taking hours of his time and he wouldn't take any payment.

Everyone remembers 'Ginge'. When he was in Year 6, his teacher's Mum's elderly dog needed a fish diet, so Ginge ensured he delivered fresh fish every week to his teacher.

These are just a few memories of unselfish, kind acts from a community of great fishermen. Long may Mevagissey enjoy and cherish such a community as this.

JUNE HAYES

CHAIRPERSON OF CHRISTMAS LIGHTS COMMITTEE

"I feel proud to be part of the Christmas Lights Committee in Mevagissey"

It was 12 years ago that June became involved with the Christmas lights. When talking to the organisers at the time, it was evident that with lack of funds and manpower the Mevagissey Lights were in danger of being permanently switched off.

"I had soon grown to love the village in the four years I had lived here and took the opportunity to get involved. With a small committee of six people, I went to the businesses in the village to ask for support and then met with the organiser of the Festival of Lights in Truro. He gave us a 13-foot lantern, *Lady of The Sea*, made from withy and willow which we had to transport from Falmouth! With the money raised we organised a lantern workshop and made small lanterns for the children to hold, so that first year we processed to the harbour for the turn on of the lights led by the *Lady of The Sea*. We then made a replica lantern of Mevagissey Lighthouse which joined subsequent processions. Due to bad weather, difficulty finding storage and low funds, the lanterns deteriorated over the years. The final blow came when on returning the lighthouse lantern to storage on the top of a car, it had become caught in a hedge. On arrival at the container all that was left was the wind arrow on top!

As a committee we decided to hold the switch-on event on the harbour, serving mulled wine and mince pies, providing entertainment for the family. When you are out there on the night of the switch-on, you see the children dancing around and people ooing and aahing when the harbour and streets are lit up, and you realise that is why you do it."

ROSE AND MIKOU DELAUNE

SHE SELLS

"Nowhere reached the expectations of Mevagissey, our dream place"

Mikou and I met in Auckland, New Zealand in 2007 whilst travelling. We fell in love and then spent five years travelling in our campervan around France, doing mainly agricultural work. Mikou is from a small fishing harbour in Normandy called Fécamp, with similar characteristics to Meva.

We decided we wanted to settle and start up a family business and while scrolling the internet we came upon a shop in beautiful Mevagissey called Apple, in Market Square. My parents, my sister, Mikou and I bought the gift shop and apartment in January 2012 and six months later renamed it 'She Sells': my Dad's suggestion as we were so close to the sea. Meanwhile, Mikou worked as manager in the pasty shop for four years.

In 2017 we jumped at the opportunity to take over our present premises on the harbour front. Initially we had half the space as a café and the other as a gift shop but when the shop next door became available, we moved the gift shop into there and enlarged our café area, expanding upstairs as well.

The fishermen come in everyday in the quieter months. One of the fishermen, Malcolm Saunders, at high tide will come and moor his boat and shout his order through the door and we will take it out to him. You could say we are a 'sail-through' as opposed to a 'drive-through'.

The last five years have been very busy. Our children Loïc and Alaïs were born, completing our family. Dave the dog, the fifth member of our family, joined us just after we moved here in 2012 and has been with us on our journey. He welcomes our customers into She Sells and is loved by all! We have enjoyed expanding our business. It has been really good for us. As Mikou says; "We live here, but it is like being on holiday everyday."

STEPH DUDLEY

CERAMIC ARTIST & FISHERMAN'S WIFE

"I now know more about fishing than I've ever thought there was to know!"

Steph refers to herself as a 'newbie' as she has only been married to Mark for five years. However, during that time she says she has learnt more about fishing, fishing gear, boat engines, weather conditions and quotas than she ever needed to know! In her new life she was soon to recognise that as a fisherman's wife there is no routine, and that being flexible is essential.

"Everything revolves around tides, weather conditions and seasonal fish. When Mark is not at sea, he is always busy, usually setting nets or doing some maintenance on the boat. Sleep is taken when needed, often during the afternoon! Luckily, I have my own pottery studio space where I can retreat. Primarily it is my hobby; I enjoy making and am fortunate to have a few outlets in local shops.

Constant new regulations in the fishing industry have made it very difficult for our fishermen. At times it can be very stressful and as a wife, I need to be very supportive.

A few years ago, I went out with Mark on one of his fishing trips. We were about six miles offshore and I decided I fancied a swim. Having jumped off the boat I then wondered how I was going to get back on board! I envisaged being towed back into the harbour like a prize catch, but in a rather undignified way Mark managed to hoist me back on board. Fishermen need be ready for all eventualities."

MARK DUDLEY

FISHERMAN

"As a fisherman you get used to your own company"

Mark has been a fisherman in Mevagissey all his life, as was his father, grandfather and great-grandfather before him. As a young lad he would take the opportunity to fish any time he was not at school. "My dad took me out fishing and in the summer holidays I would often go out in the punt by myself.

I started fishing when I was 16 and have now been fishing for 34 years. Apart from the time when I worked with my dad, Peter, I have always been a lone fisherman. You get used to your own company."

Mark fishes along the shore, usually a 20-mile stretch and no more than seven or eight miles out. "I recall once being a little too close to the shore and looking out to sea and suddenly seeing a large wave coming which filled up the boat: yes it was quite frightening!"

It is obvious that Mark enjoys fishing, particularly in the summer. "When Mevagissey is packed with people, buzzing like bees, and you go out there, to sea and it's quiet and calm, it's lovely."

PETER DUDLEY

FISHERMAN

"I still enjoy going out fishing, it's the joy of the hunt!"

Peter comes from a fishing family which dates back to the 1700s. He remembers his grandfather fishing. His son, Mark, is also a fisherman in Mevagissey.

"I have fished all my life. I first started full-time fishing at the age of 20, although I had trained as a carpenter! I worked on big luggers until my boat, *Liberty* FY43 was built in 1966. It is still in the harbour and I'm still fishing it single-handed at the age of 79!

I remember when about 70% of the boats in the harbour were family-owned, unlike the big company commercial boats of nowadays. There were no laws as such, and your boat licence was renewed yearly. There were no quotas because it was sustainable fishing; the trawling and ring netting is killing the industry. Some fishing has disappeared altogether and some come full circle."

Peter has seen the home and workplace change beyond recognition in the fact that Mevagissey used to be a total local fishing village.

"There was no-one from up town! There used to be the canning factory and fish stores on the harbour, worked by fishermen's wives. There were no second-home owners or holiday lets. People lived and worked in the village. It is a safe harbour, protected from the wind, you can go fishing no matter what the tides because of the outer pool.

Mevagissey is my home, my life, my workplace. Who needs more?"

SANDRA DUDLEY

FISHERMAN'S WIFE

"53 years a fisherman's wife and life is still much the same"

After 53 years of being married to a fisherman there is still no real routine to everyday life. Every day pans out depending on whether Peter is out fishing or not. I spend most of my time on my own. I have learnt to do things for both of us, by myself. I have had to learn to look after myself, which is fine as I am a relatively shy person and happy to keep myself to myself. I have always had animals and have loved walking the dogs. I love swimming and would spend much of my time during the finer months on the beach.

I have never worried about Peter going out to sea until the last couple of years, since his health has taken a turn for the worse. If something should go wrong for him while by himself out at sea there is no immediate help to hand. Peter has fished all his life and my son Mark learnt his skills from him at an early age. Fishing is his life and I can't see him ever giving it up altogether, despite his health, not to mention the constant changes in fishing rules, regulations and quotas. When not at sea he can be found "doing something" on his boat, *Liberty,* which just happens to be one of the oldest fishing boats in the harbour, built in 1966 in East Looe by Arthur Collins.

There are many humorous tales he could tell, not just about fishing but his life growing up in the village, so many good memories.

KATE DUDLEY

FISHERMAN'S DAUGHTER

"If you can't beat 'em, join 'em"

Superstition says it's bad luck to take a woman on board a fishing boat. Well I was only a child, so it doesn't count.

I grew up not knowing anything other than being the daughter of a fisherman. Dad was either there, in port, on the boat or at sea, whether it was a weekend, bank holiday or birthday. Fishing is my dad's life, so I thought, "If you can't beat 'em join 'em." I was about six years old the first time I went out fishing with him and I loved it, continuing to join him whenever I was able to until I left home.

I would go out in all seasons and all weather conditions, including snow. I would help shoot and pull the nets at all hours of the day and night. When very young I would have to climb into the net bin to heave the fish out. I would play tricks on my dad by looking over the side and when I saw a fish coming up would say, "I'll pull the net Dad" and take credit for pulling in the fish. He got his own back one day by attaching an octopus to my back!

Summer holidays was red mullet season and on one occasion we left the harbour late afternoon and not returning until five o'clock the next morning. No wonder I nodded off while steering the boat home!

I never had to worry about my male peers teasing me about being a fishergirl as I did everything they did and probably more. They said that I would have made a great full-time fisherman!

NICK TOMLINSON

FISHERMAN

"Angling and working my veg patch now I'm retired"

I was born in Egypt. We lived out there during the war and moved to Cornwall when I was four. "WaaHid, itneen, talaata": "one, two, three" in Arabic. My mother was teaching out there and my father was in MI5.

I went to university for a year, Royal Holloway, but academia wasn't for me. I had a mate that was deep-sea fishing out of Grimsby: I spent two years fishing out of there, then three years out of Lowestoft. I always wanted to come back to Cornwall, and as my friend Ted was working his boat *Rosa* from Plymouth I joined him. We went into a business partnership for nine years. We sold *Rosa* in the 80s and I bought a boat to do tourist trips in the summer, then worked ashore in the winter. It didn't suit me, so I bought the fishing boat *Lenten Rose* and worked her single-handed for 33 years. I'm married to Jayne and we have our son James, stepdaughter Debbie and granddaughter Gracie Mae. Enjoying retirement, some angling still and working the veg patch.

JAMES TOMLINSON

FISHERMAN

"Always told to get a trade before I go fishing"

I was always by the water, in punts and on boats, but Dad wouldn't take me on as a fisherman. He always told me to get a trade before I go fishing! After school I went to college. I lasted two terms, then I was offered a building apprenticeship.

I've worked between fishing and building, several seasons fishing with Tom Avent, some of that has been working away trips, off the ports of Brixham and Newlyn. Working between the two, I've been able to play cricket. A bit of coaching by my dad when I was younger got me hooked. I've played for Gorran Cricket Club. I've been part of the team that won the Hawkey Cup three times: it's a T20 competition for east-based clubs in Cornwall, the three top leagues. At the club and in the top leagues, we've always seen Aussies and Kiwis coming over to play for a season. Our chairman's son went out to New Zealand to play and encouraged by his experience, I went out. I ended up going out to NZ for two seasons, out in the September and back in the April. Best thing I've ever done. In 2011, our team at Gorran CC played an overseas side made up of the Kiwis and Aussies, a charity match to help support the cricket club in Christchurch, New Zealand. We raised £1,000 which helped Heathcote CC club rebuild their cricket pavilion after the major earthquakes earlier in that year.

JAYNE CROUCH

WIFE OF BOAT ENGINEER

Stuart started as an engineer on tugs on the Thames. He did live down here for a little while and that's how we met, got married and moved up to Kent where he was working on the Thames. I didn't like living up there and we moved back down and started working on Mevagissey fishing boats.

My life is much like a fisherman's wife really; any boat that's broken down has always taken priority over any plans we have had. So often the phone will ring; I dreaded it being the middle of the night, because he is so difficult to wake up! He puts the fishermen's boats first; if their boat is broken-down they can't work. Very often our plans could be cancelled at the weekend or anytime they needed him; he just went. His mind is always there; I don't think there is anybody knows as much about boats as him. Even when we are on holiday he will answer his phone and try and sort problems out. He has devoted his working life to it. I always understood that it had to be done. He has his mind on engines; he'll never retire. He loves his work.

He's come home clutching a lobster or fish someone had given him in appreciation. Stuart received a specially framed award from the Golden Maggot Committee in recognition of 30 years' service to Mevagissey Fishing Fleet. It meant a great deal to Stuart.

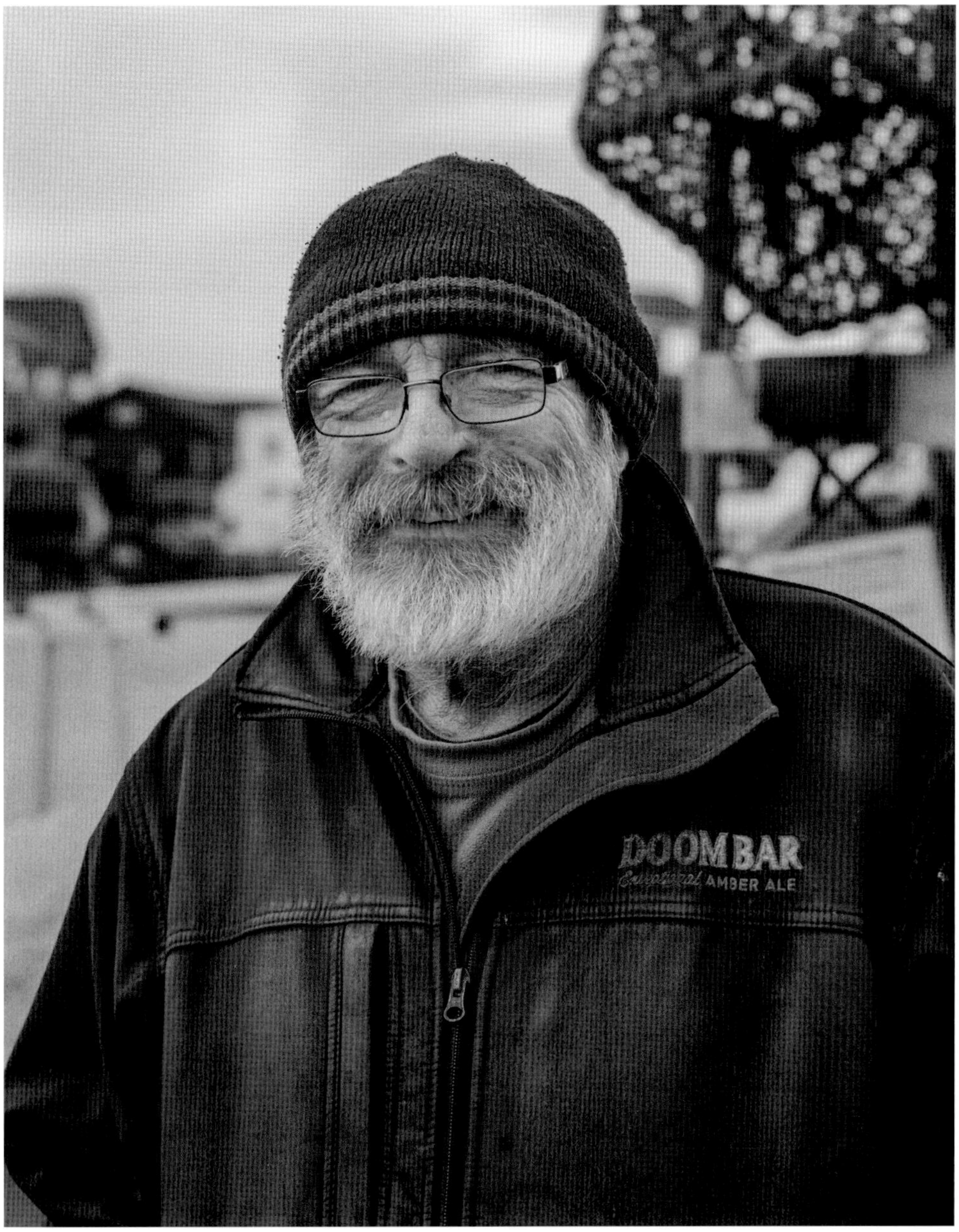

STUART CROUCH

BOAT ENGINEER

"I'm a boat fixer!"

Stuart is a modest character whose work in and around the harbour has supported the fishermen of Mevagissey for 35 years through his mechanical skills. He can often be seen on the jetty in the back of his well-kitted-out van, his mobile workshop, doing welding repairs with sparks flying!

"I have never been a fisherman but I used to work on tugs before coming here. I do engineering and welding on most of the boats in the harbour, big and small. I can be contacted any part of the day and night when fishermen have problems with their boats. Usually, I work on them in the harbour, but I have gone out on the boats if needed."

Stuart is a valuable member of the fishing community.

GERRALD CLOKE

RETIRED BUILDER

"Mevagissey: you've got the harbour, the fishermen, the heart and you've got the soul to it"

I was brought up in Mevagissey, in 1 Market Square. Father was a fisherman as was his father. My father had his own fishing boat for a while called the *Sunny Boy*, named after me! It was a small tosher. He then went on to work on different boats, one called the *Vera*. This was when he did pilchard-driving. I used to love that – it was my favourite fishing. I'd go out with him in the evening and the moon would shine on the pilchards and they looked like little jewels. Although my father went on to work in the building trade, fishing was his life really.

I went to Penrice School: I started on the day it was opened. I left there at 15 and I did a few jobs, including working in the fish factory, and then I went on to work in London in the swinging 60s where I stayed for four years. I met my wife Jackie in Newquay at a dance and the rest is history! We've been married for 53 years!

I had worked for my friend, builder Dave Churms, for a short time before I went to London and then when I returned, I worked for him from 1976 to 1985, mostly on jobs to do with the upkeep of the harbour. I remember when we used to repair the harbour wall, we used to tie a ladder to the side and climb down with a bucket and a trowel, much to the amusement of the visitors who often asked if I stepped back to admire my work!

I have always loved writing poetry and have written several including some about Mevagissey and Cornwall, my homeland.

DAVE CHURMS

RETIRED BUILDER

"People always know when I'm at the harbour because of my trademark red pick-up truck"

"I was born in London, moved to Mevagissey when I was 14 years old and went to Mevagissey High School on the hill. I wanted to be a mechanic but failed the test. It was the 'best failure' I had in my life; made me realise that success often comes from failure, a lesson that is important for youngsters to learn! I took a five-year apprenticeship as a builder and went on to work for myself. I carried out building work in Mevagissey for over 40 years, and 33 of those years were working around the harbour. When the Seagull Café was demolished by a storm in the 1970s, I had the job of rebuilding the sea wall. About 20 years ago I was working on the museum, painting. I jumped the ladder and fell off. It resulted in an air ambulance trip to Treliske!"

On examination it was found that Dave had broken two vertebrae, eight ribs and an arm! It didn't deter him and it wasn't long before he was back at work!

"When I retired I bought a small fishing boat called *Charm*. I enjoy going out with my pals mackerel fishing and if I'm lucky I might even catch a bass! Mevagissey is a wonderful place, I wouldn't live anywhere else. I've lived here for 62 years so I'm nearly a local!"

OGM – ORDER OF THE GOLDEN MAGGOT

AS TOLD BY DAVE CHURMS, FOUNDER OF THE OGM

"The fishermen say that the presentation of the Golden Maggot signifies the start of Christmas"

On the quay when I was having a fag after work, I often used to rib Freddie Turner and Graham Mills, both fishermen, about who had the biggest catch. After several weeks, Graham asked who was the winner of the biggest catch, otherwise known as the 'Maggot'. So, there marked the start of the OGM.

In 1989, I asked John Clayton, a brilliant carver of wood, who was responsible for the sign that still stands on the road as you enter the village; if I supplied the wood, would he carve out a plaque with a maggot on it? He agreed and after a few weeks it was completed. John and I formed a committee, without fishermen so it was unbiased, and included Clifford Rowe and Don Arthur. We decided we would hold the presentation on Christmas Eve with the permission of the Social Club. John not only designed the plaque but also made a gold-coloured statue, a certificate and medals, the latter of which is worn with pride on Christmas Eve. He also designed the maggot motif which is lit up every year on the Co-op along with the Christmas lights. The winner is given the Golden Maggot medal, a bottle of whisky and a framed certificate and has their photograph displayed alongside the plaque for the year.

In order to be nominated you need to have either: the biggest catch; have saved a life or lives; made a 'cock-up'; or raised a large amount of money for charity. My daughter Louise did the typing and paperwork for several years until Matt Rowe followed in his father's footsteps and became a committee member and has continued with this role. I hand out diaries to certain fishermen and people around the harbour, to make notes in the course of the year and Lauren Hunkin has collected the nominations and stories for some years. Without her collecting the stories there would be no Golden Maggot!

Our first winner was the late Freddie Turner who with other boats was going out fishing to raise money for charity; he merely missed the tide, got stuck in the mud and had to be towed into deeper water, much to the amusement of onlookers. Needless to say, a large amount of money was raised for charity! At the presentation there was lots of whisky supplied. Marion Clayton made sausage rolls and mince pies; my wife Maggie took the photographs and has done so every year since and a good deal of paperwork behind the scenes. Dr Hanan would present the trophies yearly and after his passing, his wife Dorothy took over. We have had different main speakers including John Arthur, Don Arthur, Graham Mills and Malcolm Saunders, known affectionately as Animal. Joe Chesterfield, Mevagissey's answer to Jethro, is our present speaker. Peter Clayton organises the drinks for the event and the engraving for the Maggot with money raised. Gerald Goode always did a great job with collecting money!

The committee is now made up of Matt Rowe, Paul Wakeling, Julian Barron and myself. Without everyone doing their part, it wouldn't be the success that it is today.

The Social Club is packed on Christmas Eve for the presentation of the Golden Maggot, not just with fishermen but their wives, friends and family. They say that this is the start of Christmas.

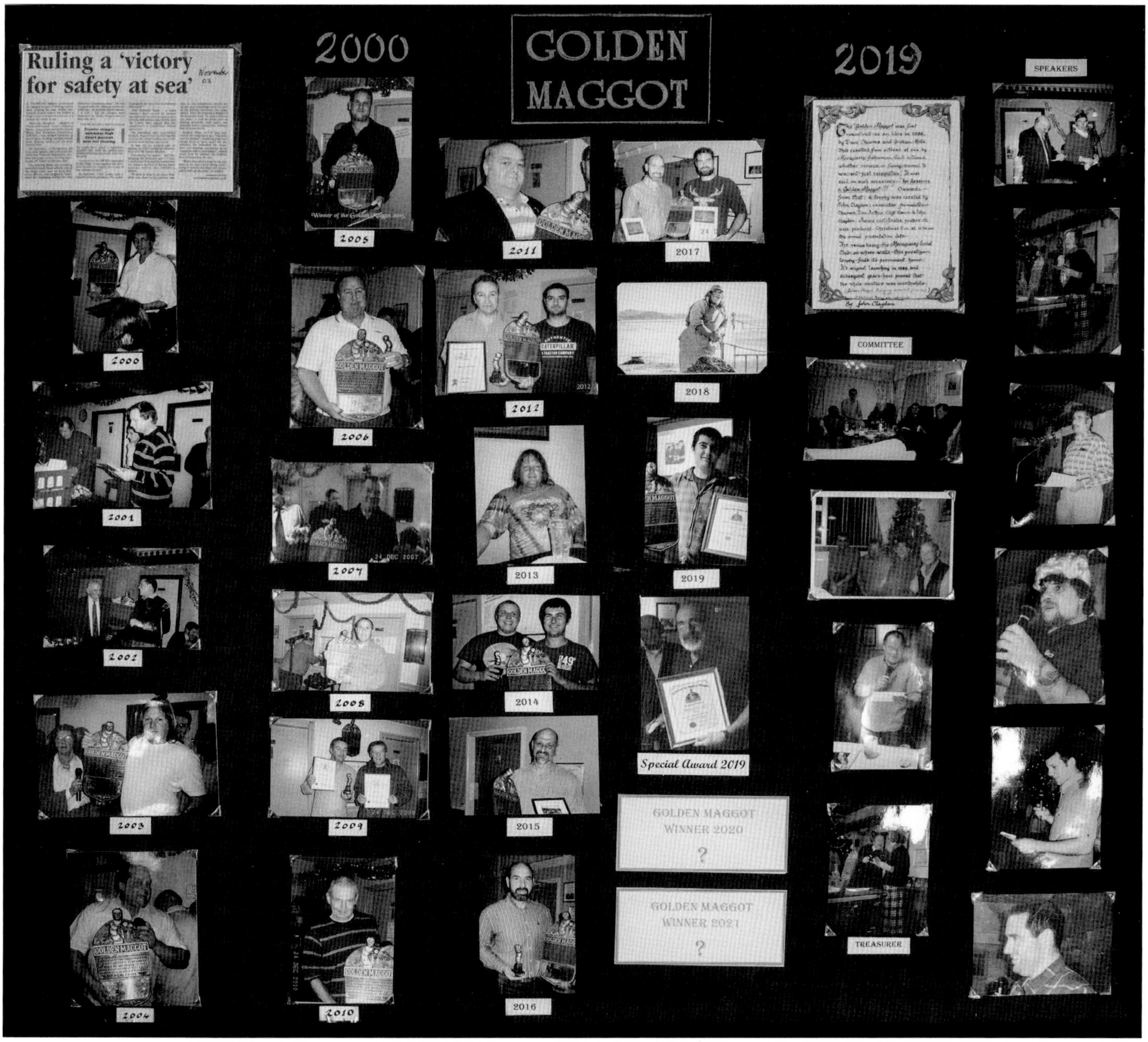

JOE CHESTERFIELD

SKIPPER & FISHERMAN

Hi I'm Joe. I'm an owner/skipper out of Mevagissey. My family has been fishing out of Mevagissey for several generations and since leaving school I've been trawling for the last 18 years on the family boat and two years ago I broke away from the family and bought my own boat which I continue to be trawling and netting on daily. I have a very understanding wife and two crazy kids and have lived in Meva all my life. There really is no other job like it in the world from rough seas to beautiful sunrises and from days where we barely cover our diesel to other days when we fill every box we've got; fishing really is like Forest Gump's box of chocolates.

Mevagissey has a very successful fishing community for a small port and more youngsters are interested in following in their family's footsteps here than the average port. It's a really friendly and thriving port with plenty happening every day. All the fishing ports I've been, I've never found one I would rather fish out of. Unlike some ports there is a wide variety of fishing that happens from here from crabbing and trawling to scalloping, seine netting, and static netting as well as a fleet of hand liners. I absolutely love my job and plan to continue fishing long past my retirement age.

AMANDA CHESTERFIELD

FISHERMAN'S WIFE

"My husband says 'it's a job for love not money'"

The photos make fishing look heaven; blue skies and flat seas. Living each week, hand to mouth, relying on nature to be kind with the forecasts. Many young men have tried fishing and left again, because of the inconsistent income. But that is the nature of the job. Joe will say it's in his blood and there's no other job he would do.

When you are raising a family it's a hard job to accept as a wife. He can be home a straight week, which is great for the family but it means no wages! Taking time off for a holiday means no wages, fitting in dentist, doctor, or hospital appointments means no wages. So often he just carries on with his health complaints, as he can't afford to be in from sea. Some weeks you shop well; other weeks, we have learnt to make things stretch.

The children complain that daddy's never here and you try to explain it's because he loves us and works hard to pay the bills and buy the things you want and need. When he started working longer trips away, it was hard all round; it's hard living as a single parent during that time, doing everything and holding it all together with nobody to chat to when the kids are in bed, it's lonely. They know he goes away to sea and they know when he'll be back, and in the meantime; it's the 'three musketeers' at home.

DAVID CHESTERFIELD
FISHERMAN

"Hiya Dave, welcome home"

I'd scull out to a punt and lay the nets for the night whilst I was at school, I always knew I'd go fishing. In the summer I'd look after the family's boat hire business and fish at night and fish more in the winter. Born in Mevagissey; father's side were all fishermen. Grandfather was a fisherman and a sail-maker in the village, great-grandfather sailed on the Cutty Sark.

We've always worked a boat; my brother Ed and I bought a share into the family boat back in 84/85, the *Francis* 45-foot wooden hull boat. Then some years later we travelled up to Stornoway to buy the 40-foot boat *Ocean Harvest*. It took three long days to sail her back home. Now I'm working a smaller boat, 21-foot Cygnus called *Sunshine*.

I've been visiting the Greek isles since I was young and my wife Shirley and I visit Zante every year. As long as I'm by a harbour and a taverna, I'm happy. Shirley says, "Bleddy hell look, boats again, even if we are top of a mountain you'd still look out for a harbour." In the suitcase is a telescopic rod. I'm then often in the harbour, catching fish and talking with the fishermen. We've got to know many people and still keep in touch; we're honoured to eat with families and I've cooked fish in a restaurant. It's a high compliment when you arrive and land at the port and the locals say, "Hiya Dave, welcome home."

CHRIS CHESTERFIELD

FISHERMAN

The Chesterfield family has worked on boats stretching back to the time of the Cutty Sark. In 1922, the clipper was towed back to Falmouth from Portugal where it had been rotting on the mudflats. Chris's grandfather, Joseph George Martin Chesterfield, was in charge of her transformation back to square rig in preparation to become a training ship for boys entering the navy or becoming seamen. A photo of his grandfather on the poop deck hangs proudly in Chris's home. His great-uncle, Martin Chesterfield, had the job of measuring and making the sails for the ship, requiring climbing the masts which was quite scary! He also embroidered a cloth for the pulpit of the old Wesleyan Chapel which is now on display in St Andrew's Church.

Chris's life as a fisherman was very different! "I used to go out on the family boat, the *Cristabel* with my dad, Joe Chesterfield, from the age of about three and would spend as much time as I could, including school holidays and weekends, fishing – and any other opportunity I had to go out to sea!

When I left school in 1975, the family sold the *Cristabel* and bought another boat called the *Francis* and I joined David and Edwin, my cousins, along with their father, William, my father Joe and one other crew member. I worked on the family boat up to 1978. My Dad retired but continued making my nets in his garden until he was 95! At this time, I went on my own, having different boats, doing various methods of fishing; anything from crabbing to trawling, to fly seining and wreck netting. I'd always wanted to work in the North Sea on the really big boats so in 1990 I went up there to the Shetland Islands and helped out Freddie Turner (also a Mevagissey fisherman). I stayed there for six years before returning to Mevagissey.

In 2003, I owned a smaller boat and one day when I was at sea, the boat took a couple of waves and it was a strong wind and I was blown overboard. The boat sank and I was in the water for eight hours, firstly swimming and then drifting around with the tide to save energy. I was rescued by the helicopter. It was October and the temperature was 14 degrees. They reckon I was lucky to have survived in the water that long. I was in Treliske hospital for a week and then when I came out, I went straight back to sea. They say, "Jump back on the horse when you fall off", so that's what I did!

I now own the trawler *Breaking Dawn* and I am one of the oldest working fishermen in Mevagissey!"

SUSAN CHESTERFIELD

FISHERMAN'S WIFE

"Chris doesn't like being on land, he's better off at sea"

"I was born in West Bridgford in Nottingham, we were all the 'Boots' family. Grandparents, Mum and Dad all worked for Boots, the major employer at the time in Nottingham. My mum and dad, Michael and Mary Charles had the opportunity to buy a successful lacemaking company in the city. They had about 40 outworkers, and supplied lace to companies including Birkin and Charnos. So I joined the business when I left school and continued until we moved down here in 1998 with my former husband and our three children. Mum and Dad then sold the business and the house and followed a year later. They never looked back." Mary still lives in Cliff Street. Sadly Michael passed away in 2020 but she loves Mevagissey and the people love her. She regularly sits on the harbour with a morning coffee supplied by She Sells as she watches life around the busy harbour.

"After my marriage broke up, I met Chris who I then married and we had three children.

2003 was a bad year. We lost our son Caden who was still born. Later that year Chris sank his boat at sea. I remember visiting him in intensive care and all he could say was, 'Can you get me the charts as I need to get back to sea.' Whereupon he discharged himself and went straight back on the boat! He doesn't like being on land, he's better off back at sea!

We have two daughters, Tegen, 20 and Bracken, 15. Tegen was never interested in fishing unlike her sister. When Bracken was younger, she enjoyed going out with her dad fishing"

Bracken: "I used to go out with Dad quite a lot as soon as I knew how to swim properly, probably most weekends but then a year ago I went off fish and didn't want to go anymore! I didn't like trawling, it's just not fun and you have to wait around. The only time I liked going out was when he would do the cuttlefish pots and the wrasse pots, 'cos' they were fun. I did cuttlefish day-care; I would clean the ink off them and put them in the boxes with the ice and look after them while Dad was setting up the new baskets. I'm not sure what I want to do yet. I have another year left in school. My sister, Tegen is enjoying her work as a carer." Bracken and Tegen are not set to follow their Dad into the fishing industry!

JIMMY ROWE

RETIRED BUILDER

"I've always been around the village, being a menace most of the time!"

"My grandparents and parents lived in Mevagissey. I was brought up in the village with my two brothers and sister. My father had a hardware stall in St Austell in the Market House. I started school on the same day as Kev Evans and we have been friends ever since!

When I left school, I went on to do a building apprenticeship and after serving my time as an apprentice bricklayer, I went wherever there was work. I worked for Wimpey for 33 years, where I had progressed through the company and then after taking early retirement, I worked for myself helping with the building of many big houses in the village. I have always lived in Mevagissey and worked away for weeks at a time whenever necessary, mostly in the West Country, but always returning home. I've always worked hard and played hard!

I have had boats all my life but never wished to become a full-time fisherman. I enjoy going out with my mates fishing for pleasure. I have a boat in the boatyard at Portmellon. It is the oldest boat to have been in the harbour. Built in 1927, it is a Mevagissey tosher, a 20-foot wooden boat named *My Julie*, which I have now been working on for 15 years! I have renewed 50 of the ribs, the stern and bow and I have a new engine ready to fit."

In Cornish terms, Jimmy will have the boat back in the water 'dreckly'.

"I also have always had a love of motorbikes and have had many through the years. I used to have a motorbike and sidecar. I replaced the sidecar with a flat board with a settee on the back! I remember picking my mother up in the village with her shopping and taking her home up Tregoney Hill, she ended up screaming as her dress ballooned up in the air. Despite her shouts to slow down, I drove even faster. I was a bit of a menace in my younger days!"

KEVIN EVANS

RETIRED FISHERMAN

"An old mine on board... my position? I am on my knees praying!"

Kev Evans came to Mevagissey in 1974 and worked with Colin Williams for seven years on several of his trawlers before buying his own boat.

"The fishing industry was very different then. There were few restrictions on what you could catch, you didn't need a licence and crew members didn't need certificates, you just did the job. I wouldn't be able to go back in the fishing industry now without doing several courses.

One day in August we were trawling down off The Dodman. The sea was flat calm. We picked up a huge metal cylinder. It was so heavy, we managed to get it on board but had to cut the trawl to take a closer look. I thought it was a mooring buoy at first but the crew soon came to the conclusion it was an old war mine! We rang the coastguard who told us to not allow it to get hot and to keep hosing it down till we returned to the bay. I was asked our position. My reply was that I was on my knees praying! We arrived back in the bay, just off Pentewan beach where we were met with the Mine Disposal Squad. It turned out that there was 800lbs of explosives in the mine! We pushed it over the side and it sunk to the sea bed. When it was detonated, it shook the windows in the village of Pentewan and on the Pentillie estate." Kev and his crew had a lucky escape!

Kev's trawler fishing was quite eventful. Not long after the mine incident, he 'caught' a dummy torpedo which again had to be brought ashore and disposed of safely by the Navy. Then there was the story of part of an old shipwreck that became entangled! Nowadays Kev enjoys going out with his mates in a smaller vessel, fishing for pleasure. No mines, torpedoes or wrecks!

MARCUS HUNKIN

NETRIGGER

"Fishing is an honest day's work, for an honest day's pay"

"I loved working on the boats as a fisherman but I became a bag of nerves out there against the elements, in all conditions, deprived of sleep, physically hard work. It wasn't good experiencing panic attacks out at sea and I realised I needed to come ashore. I had one or two scary moments out at sea but I don't know what actually triggered the panic attacks! I had a good skipper, who was really supportive but I had to stop. I miss it and the camaraderie – it's tight. There is no fire brigade or ambulance – we just relied on each other out there."

While working on the nets he often goes over his years as a fisherman; day-dreaming about one day owning and running his own boat. Knowing he'll never get a boat but it's all nice happy thoughts. "I think of all the fishermen no longer with us, in happier times, and still miss them on a daily basis, but think of the good times with them.

As a net maker I repair and make the nets for mainly two boats and fit in and around the rest of the fleet in Mevagissey. Wreck nets in winter until Easter, and then work on trammel nets, ray nets, mackerel nets, bass nets, sole nets – only thing I don't make is onion nets! I put my headphones on and I am lost in my own world, as I work away on the nets on my own."

PETER JENKINS

RETIRED FISHERMAN

"Helen and I built my sailing dinghy on the harbour 40 years ago"

I was born and brought up in Mount Wise, now part of Plymouth. My earliest memories are of Hitler trying to kill me, during the many bombing raids of the second world war! My mother's family was from St Ives, and my father's from Kingsand on the Rame Peninsula, on the Cornish side of Plymouth Sound. After the war we spent a lot of time in Kingsand and I was allowed out in a boat on my own from the age of seven. After leaving school I worked in the Dockyard, still fishing in the evenings and at weekends. A couple of years on I went into the Merchant Navy, where I became very familiar with offshore pipelines – although I did meet someone from St Austell in Venezuela once, on a rare trip ashore! I then joined the RAF Marine Craft Section (MCS), became a coxswain, and served in Aden. When the MCS was disbanded I decided to go fishing full-time, and had a series of boats, trawling, scalloping, netting etc.

I moved to Mevagissey in the 1970s when I met my future wife, Helen. In the 1980s I spent a few years skippering survey boats in Abu Dhabi and Dubai, but then returned to Mevagissey and fishing once again. Now I sail the 16-foot sailing dinghy which Helen and I built on the harbour forty years ago, and we carry mackerel lines with us, just in case!

AZA ADLAM

ARTIST

After many visits to Cornwall since buying a little caravan on retirement, Aza, formerly an adult education art and craft tutor, decided to make the village her home in 2015.

One of the first people I met was Bill Barron, an 85-year-old gentleman who was one of the founder members of the Social Club. We would meet up once a week when he would make me one of his special coffees (no milk but a generous dash of Irish cream liqueur). He introduced me to the Club, insisting I stood at the bar with him rather than "hang around at the edges" and so through him I met many local people who frequented it. Soon I started to run stained glass workshops there and they even created a craft room on the upper floor which I equipped with a variety of craft tools and materials for members to use.

I became involved, through our local councillor, with community projects such as clearing the cemetery and other areas around the village. Through doing this we came across some graffiti on the shelter half way up the cliff path. We subsequently painted over this in white and then I painted a sea scene. It was the first time I had ever painted anything larger than a miniature!

This started what became something of a trail of murals comprising flora, fauna and fishing boats around the village: on the bus stop; a wall up the path of Shilly Alley Op; various private house walls; and, more famously, the butterfly wall in Willow Car Park in connection with the 'Parking for Pollinators' campaign. I also painted the lower cabins of the boat *Seascan* with fishing boats and sea creatures."

Aza's many fabric journals depict the sea, sealife, the natural world and her visits to places around Cornwall and include embroidery, paintings, sketches, poems and even shipping forecasts!

Her love for Cornwall, and in particular her home in Meva, is evident through all of her range of artworks, and she continues to teach here and, she hopes, inspire others.

PHILIP GARDINER

POTTER

"I was offered the position of manager of the Pentewan Pottery in 1971 but I really wanted to be on the wheel and after four years I got a position back in Stoke as Head Thrower; that's all I wanted to do was sit at the wheel throwing. But after eight years we could afford to return to Mevagissey and be a potter where the fruit and veg shop is now, which is very small but it got us here!"

I knew Mevagissey was good for trade and I do believe there are only three ways to sell studio pottery: by name; middle of a city; or tourist destination. We went to the bank manager and bought my present studio/shop and never looked back. It's a job and a hobby and not one of those things where I think, "Oh I've got to go to work." I work through from Easter until end of November while supplying pottery to the National Trust shops for the whole of the South West and have supplied to quite a few establishments over the years, but now as I am so established, I work mainly from the shop.

A lot of my regular customers come back time after time, maybe every two or three years and buy a few pots. I've always maintained that I want to do my work on the wheel; everything is by hand to ensure it's all handmade pottery. I just want to be a one-man potter.

ROB CONSTANTINE

HARBOUR VOLUNTEER BEACH CLEANER

"I hope my work makes a difference. Keeping the harbour clean and tidy brings a smile to my face"

Rob first visited Mevagissey in the 1970s but it wasn't until he retired that, with his longing to return to the sea, he and his wife came to live in the village nearly three years ago. He left his nursery and garden centre business in Crediton, Devon and crossed the border into Cornwall!

"I first became involved with beach cleaning on Polstreath beach, which is situated below my house. I also took an interest in a new project, the Three Bays Wildlife set up by Jeremy Roberts, which primarily studies the wildlife in the Cornish area. One of their initiatives is beach cleaning on local beaches including Pentewan, Vault, Porthluney and the harbour. These take place twice a year, namely Spring and Autumn. I felt there needed to be some continuity in the harbour so that rubbish did not build up, particularly in the tourist season, so I took it upon myself to monitor and as time permitted, keep the place clean and tidy. I hate seeing polythene bags and beer cans floating on the water and hopefully I help to prevent this. Currently I go down twice a week."

Rob can be spotted, picker-up in one hand, black bag in the other!

"Much of the rubbish I pick up is historic, has been there many years and has gradually found its way to the surface." Rob was particularly aware this year that there were fewer plastic spoons, forks, straws etc. which shows how the local businesses are becoming more environmentally friendly.

"I enjoy doing the beach cleaning. It brings a smile to my face and I often have a good 'chin-wag' with the fishermen."

TOM DORAN

FISHERMEN'S CHIPPY

"With the fishing industry on our doorstep, it's a great benefit. By connecting our fish and chips to the sea, it holds a magic. We receive positive feedback from our customers because of it"

Our main staple is cod and haddock; we use about 100 kilograms a day which come from Icelandic waters, which our fishermen don't catch from. But the other species that appear seasonally from Mevagissey fishermen, such as whiting or scallops, we buy fresh from them. We run 'Fish Specials' to use the local fish, including fish cakes.

We aim to produce a high-quality product and the reason it gets so well enjoyed by our customers, is they can eat them on the quay and see the boats bring their load of fish in. A lot of fishermen are our customers. We enjoy the vast array of different characters and they're our best customers for haddock; most of the tourists go for cod. We are trading off a small mobile van too now and hope to cater for parties, campsites and weddings in the summer, with the van.

Our packaging for the takeaway food is ecologically sourced too now in 'bio-trays', made of pulp and fully recyclable, and the paper too; being by the sea it has a greater meaning to the environment and our business.

PAUL WAKELING

EX-FISHERMAN

"Going out in the middle of the night and coming back three days later. Fishing is a primal experience; a spiritual sensation"

Paul moved to Mevagissey in 1981 and became a fisherman. "The first boat was *John Edge*, a 32-foot open-decked wooden boat and the skipper was John Lee. We had shot the nets, which had to be left for ten hours before hauling them. It was a bright, sunny, Sunday afternoon, in the middle of the English Channel, and we had tankers and ferries passing us either side. We'd cooked a full roast dinner, less the red wine, and sat on the deck, enjoying our roast dinner! Brilliant! I also worked on the *Legionnaire*, *Jean Nancy* and *Sea Spray*, to name a few, in the ten years I was a fisherman in Mevagissey.

I moved back up to Surrey and opened a mobile fish shop, and bought all my fish from Mevagissey fishermen and Plymouth, selling it fresh to customers and restaurants in Surrey, until I had an accident with the van and it ended upside-down in the harbour!

So I then opened a shop called 'Cornwall Fish' selling salt water crabs, until 2001, when I moved back to Mevagissey and started my business in a new venture: fixing chimneys.

I have seen a lot of fishermen struggle over the years, and see a generation gap with fishing today, due to the decimation of fishing in Britain. But it's great there are so many young fishermen working in Mevagissey harbour. Its Harbour Trustees are doing a good job for the harbour; it's tidy and clean and keeps its uniqueness, and history, like the three holes in the harbour wall created for the guns against the Germans in WWII. The holes were for three guns, but only ever had one bullet! That's the character of Mevagissey."

CHRIS GILL

AQUILA CHARTERS

"I suffered with seasickness as a child!"

I was five years old when I started fishing on the boats in the harbour. I would go out either on my father's boat *An-Balores*, the *Penair* with Jack Lean, or with Martin Carrington on the *Aquila*. I suffered from seasickness every time I went out as a child and was 14 before I had my first sick-free day! The feeling of catching soon outweighed the feeling of seasickness.

I did not live in Mevagissey as a child so I spent much of my time fishing in the River Fal at Tresillian, always racing home from school to dig worms and get to the best spot before my mates. Then at the weekends, my father would take me out on the boat.

At 28 I got the opportunity to work the *Aquila*. After Harvey John had a near-fatal accident at work, he decided to have a change of occupation, bought the *Aquila* and asked me to work her with him. I jumped at the chance, doing all my tickets to become skipper in 2005. A couple years later he sold me the business, handlining mackerel as a commercial fisherman and chartering the rest of the time. I spent time trying different types of commercial fishing, longlining, and netting with differing success. The most successful I've been is with my chartering, shark fishing and now big game. In 2016 Atlantic bluefin tuna started to reappear in the waters off Mevagissey. Since then, I have worked on both learning to catch them and lobbying to get the UK quota. In 2021 the UK got quota and I was issued one of 15 licences to catch, tag and release on the UK's CHART programme, successfully catching almost 200 up to the end of 2021. I'm currently lobbying to get a saleable quota for us as the South West Handline Fishermen's Association.

STEWART EAST

FISHERMAN

"There is something special about Mevagissey, because we all know each other"

I was in the Duke of Cornwall Infantry and came with my army pal to Mevagissey on leave and met my wife, who was a daughter of a fisherman, and he showed me how to fish. So I tried sea fishing. It turned out he was hopeless at plummet fishing, and I was really good at it. It's where you have two wooden booms with a line coming off each and a 3lb lead weight and a spinner, and you can catch a lot of mackerel, even when it's scarce. My best catch was 29 stone of mackerel in four hours; they came in one at a time and took some work to do. It was 1964, and I needed a second job when I married and had a young family; I enjoyed the challenge of fishing. They used to sell mackerel then by the foot, not the weight because they were long and thin.

Years ago there would always be a dozen fishermen walking up and down the quay at any time of the day. Those days have gone because the youngsters are forced to live outside the fishing harbour with so many incomers and second homes. Those days are gone forever.

LEWIS KEMP

FISHERMAN

"I was always a keen sea angler and out fishing with my dad with the rods and interested in the sea and had the opportunity to move down. Fishing was always something I wanted to do and was lucky enough to get a job working for Brackan Pearce on the *Spirited Lady III*"

I did the sea survival course to get my licence but was really fortunate to go on the RNLI sea survival course and that opened my eyes to how important it is to wear the new lifejackets supplied to us. It certainly proved to me how a matter of life and death they are if you fell in the sea – without it on I lasted 55 seconds before sinking to the bottom of the wave pool. I was still afloat after 15 minutes with the life jacket on. It was really a worthwhile course to have experienced, really informative; I wear it religiously.

Now as I am talking to you, I'm heading home and watching dolphins swim beside the boat. I love seeing what's in the nets as we bring them up – I am like a little kid. It reminds me of looking in rock pools as a kid and being mesmerised and still am really. You never know what to expect fishing; whether it will be a good catch or not or seeing a sunset, or the bow of the boat smashing through a 40-foot wave. There can be days we have no sleep at all on board. It's certainly physically challenging.

TONY PEARCE

RETIRED FISHERMAN

"There's an old saying 'Gear before beer!' because you've got to prepare, stock or work on your boat all the time, 24/7"

Before chart plotter computer programmes, we had a graph book and what was called a 'Decca Mk 4' [navigator], where we'd read our position off three clocks and refer that back to the graph book to tell us exactly where we were at sea. I started as a fisherman in Plymouth on an old Belgian trawler, British-owned called the *Pinto* and I learnt all my skills. I moved to Mevagissey in 1972 and in 1976 I purchased the *Tudor Owen II* and worked that for many years from Mevagissey harbour, until I got married and moved to St Just in 1999. I worked the *Tudor Owen II* from Newlyn and fished from Mevagissey during the winter for the lemon sole season.

When I retired, I handed my boat over to my son Brackan, 19 years old, with an experienced crew member who was a similar age to me who would keep an eye on him and help him out. Brackan has worked up from there and become a brilliant fisherman.

The Fishermen's Mission did a medical referral to Dreadnought [medical service] for me to have my hip replacement; I am now awaiting my second new hip.

A crewman wanted a 'trip off' and we went to sea two-handed without him and caught nearly four tons of bass! We were allowed to land them then and on the quay he asked, "How'd you get on?" We showed him our catch and he started crying – for us it was a bumper catch! Unfortunately now we have to dump all bass caught back in dead!

I am now working with the Newlyn Harbour Commissioners and apply all my fishing knowledge and skill and I work with everybody.

BRACKAN PEARCE

FISHERMAN

"Every day is different with fishing – you have the good times to be able to cope with the bad times, to make it worth it. One of the best was when my own boat was launched. It was a big event for me at the age of 19"

I've been around fishing all my life through my father being a fisherman and when I was 14 years old my dad bought a small boat we used in Newlyn Harbour and I progressed from that to working on fishing boats in Mevagissey. At the age of 17, I started trawling with my dad, and after a couple weeks Dad's back was hurting and he said, "Well you can take the boat son." I said, "But I've only been doing it a couple weeks?" "You'll be alright!" From that I went from being partner of my own boat to being a skipper/owner of *Spirited Lady*, a purpose-built twin rig trawler, by the age of 19. There's a crew of two besides myself. It was challenging and I worked at making it work, with a lot of effort. It just seemed to come naturally to me; I love fishing else I just couldn't do it, and hope to introduce my son to fishing too.

We work lots of bad weather. It's a modern boat built for the job so it's quite capable of coping with various conditions at sea. Rough seas don't bother me but it's never comfortable at the time but it's all part of it. We try to go about our day-to-day operations on deck as if every day is bad weather; we secure everything on board and are tied in as a matter of discipline – you have to be! Even when it's fine. So when it is bad weather it's not a shock to the system. So we do the same thing every day regardless.

You can't beat it when you come home and your son runs up to you on the jetty and hugs you. Doesn't matter how tired and weary you feel: it's special.

ALICE CLOKE

FISHERMAN'S WIFE

"I asked our son Charlie, 'What's the best and the worst thing about Daddy being a fisherman?' and he said, 'The best thing about Daddy being a fisherman is you can have loads of smoked Haddock. The worst thing about Daddy being a fisherman is he has to stay away quite a lot.' And that just about sums it up!"

I come from one of the oldest fishing families in Mevagissey, but if you told me ten years ago that I would end up married to a fisherman, I'd have either laughed or cried!!

To me, fishermen were always stinky, bearded men, hanging around on the harbour and definitely not for me! That was until I met Brackan mending nets on the quay nine years ago, and the rest is history.

It's not easy being a 'fisher WAG' as we call it (fisher wives and girlfriends!). In the first couple of years of our relationship, people thought that I made Brackan up; he was always at sea and I would go to parties, weddings, and funerals alone – that's the way it is in a fishing family.

On the flip side of that, every moment not spent at sea is precious and family time is everything to us. The excitement for our five year-old son Charlie when Daddy is coming home from sea is palpable and sometimes if the boat is having jobs done or the weather is bad, we can have several days at home together which is very special to us.

The fact that statistically one in every 20 fisherman dies at sea is never far from our thoughts, and every time Brackan leaves to go to sea, it flashes through my mind, but I try to push it to the back of my thoughts and get on with the day ahead.

ANGIE CLOKE

WIFE OF SKIPPER JOHN CLOKE

"During January 1974 I had such a shock! My fiancé, local fisherman and skipper John Cloke, fondly known as 'Clokie', came home in a right panic; he had taken a phone call of grave significance... he told me he could lose his new fishing boat!"

What happened was: Clokie had made a decision to 'go bigger' so had sold his 28-foot tosher named *Aquarius*, and ordered a Halmatic 36-foot, a fibreglass hull, moulded in yellow and manufactured in the Orkneys. At that time all the fishing boats in Mevagissey harbour were timber-constructed, so she was somewhat revolutionary!

The boat had recently been delivered as a bare hull to be fitted out at Weymarine, Weymouth. Work began: the deck-beams, port gunwale and part of the wheelhouse got built... then the boatyard went bust! Hence the phone call from Morris Molem, the foreman at the yard.

Thankfully, understanding the potential repercussions, Morris acted quickly and moved the hull out of the yard on a lorry just in time before the court bailiffs could seize her!

Having been retrieved, she was taken from Weymouth to Ferry Bridge Boatyard at Portland Harbour where work recommenced. The delay was costly as in addition to losing the earlier stage payments, a season's fishing was lost. This was very stressful to us at that time but eventually, *Angelle Marie* (named after me), arrived in Mevagissey harbour. Along with crew Albert Moreford and Frank Quinton, equipped with gurdy and strippers, *Angelle Marie* fished for mackerel during the winter months and longlining during the summer months, until 1976 when Clokie decided once again to 'go bigger' and she was traded up and out of the harbour.

GORDON STUART

AN EARLY MEMBER OF THE SEA ANGLING CLUB & HARBOUR TRUSTEE

Mum and Dad moved down to Mevagissey and before Dad could unpack any boxes, he had a heart attack. I was working for Vickers Armstrong Aircraft but I left my job to help the family move in. I had two weeks out of work then was asked to join Teddington Controls in St Austell. The company was originally based in Middlesex but at the time the government offered a ready-to-move-in factory deal. I spent the next 24 years working there in production and later visiting clients.

I retired at 64 and spent more time enjoying hobbies with my wife Shirley. We'd go sailing around the coast, up to Devon and over to the Scillies. I was an early member of the Sea Angling Club, there in the early days of wreck fishing, catching interesting varieties of fish with Bernard Hunkin and taking out an interested BBC journalist.

Shirley was the founder member of the Friends of the Surgery. She needed a heart monitor for a few days and the machine had to come from Treliske hospital. The surgery couldn't afford the equipment and so Shirley and her friends raised money and within eight years the surgery was well equipped. Sadly, Shirley passed away a few years ago. My adult daughter Amanda Jane lives in Twickenham and son James Edward in Worle near Weston-super-Mare.

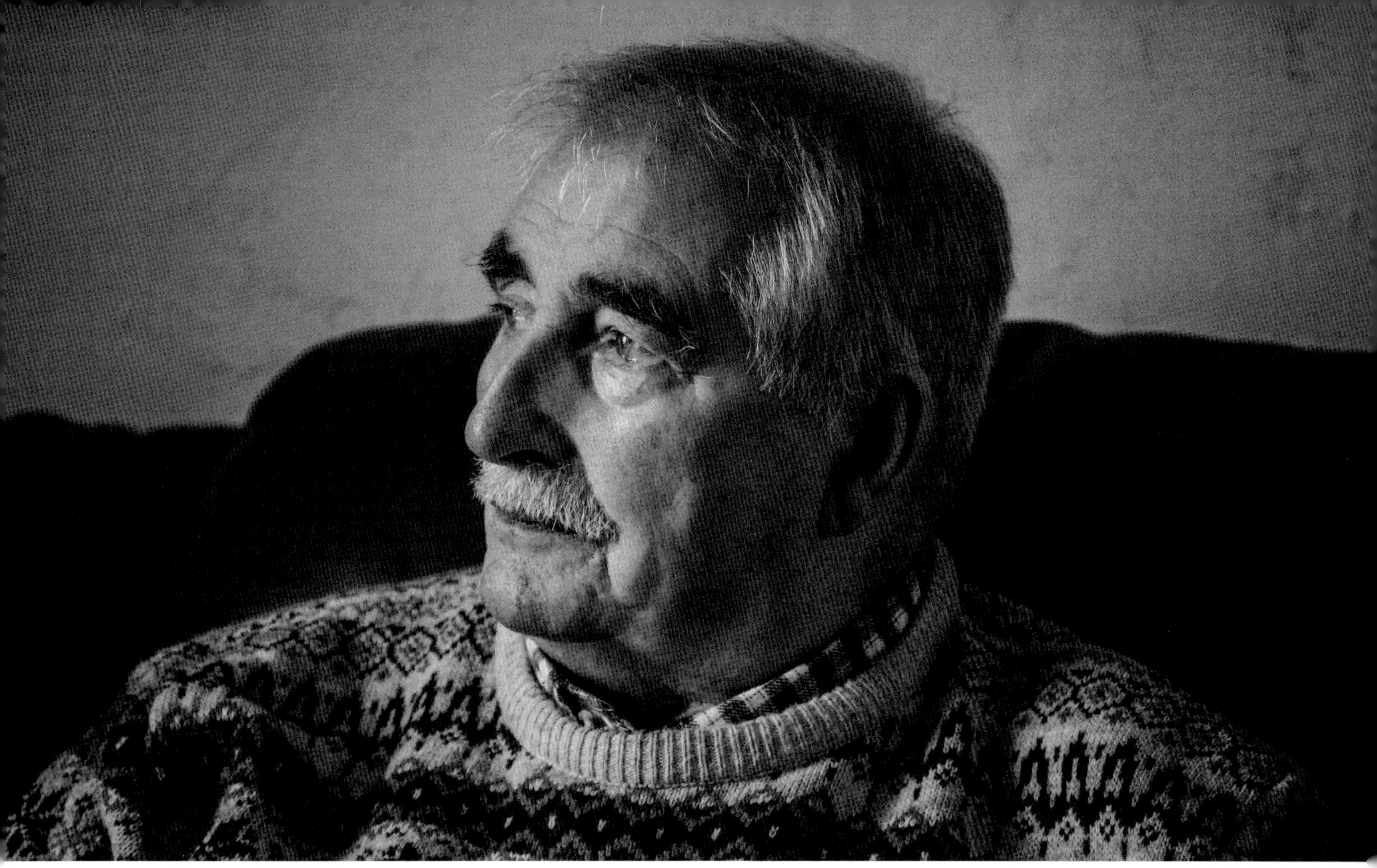

JOHN ARTHUR

RETIRED FISHERMAN

"'Fishing is a curious uncertainty', a phrase adopted by John from a famous Looe fisherman, Alfred John Pengelly"

John grew up in a fishing family. In 1905 his grandfather, Alf Thomas, concerned that he could not see his boat in the harbour from his house, decided to purchase the house on The Cliff where John grew up and still lives today.

"I have been a fisherman for 56 years, only retiring last November at the age of 77. I enjoyed taking holidaymakers on the half-hour trips around the bay. In 1962 there were 44 boats in Mevagissey licensed to carry passengers; nowadays there are only six.

One event which stays in my memory is when in 1975 I was fishing with my mate off Falmouth. In those days there was no GPS. We were fishing for mackerel, busy grading them, when ahead about ¾ mile (I had good eyesight), I saw something bobbing up and down. Dismissed by my mate, I carried on with my work. Suddenly an orange flare appeared in the sky and emerging alongside the boat was a 5,000-ton nuclear submarine! It frightened the living daylights out of me!

Fishing is unpredictable. I recall once, longline fishing with a eight- or nine-mile line, 1500 hooks and 20 stone of mackerel as bait, we brought in 13 fish! The next day using the same equipment we brought in a ton and a half of fish. That's why the phrase "fishing is a curious uncertainty" is so true.

In 2004, Prince Edward opened the Activity Centre in Mevagissey. As Parish Councillor I was asked to take him by boat from the harbour to Portmellon for a reception. Not wishing to miss out on free food and drink, I arranged for my friend to drive the boat back. Needless to say, I needed a taxi back home!

The harbour has been my whole life. It is the core of Mevagissey, unable to be altered due to conservation and listed buildings preventing change. It won't ever lose its character.

BRIAN BALL

SKIPPER OF THE CHARLOTTA

"Looking back I should have become a porn star!"

At the age of 15 – dressed like Johnny Rotten – I left school, moved from Brixham to Plymouth to live with my sister and brother-in-law and started fishing full-time with my brother-in-law. Fishing has been my life ever since.

It was whilst landing our daily catch in Mevagissey that I met my long-suffering wife (who I am told countless times deserves a medal or two!) Roll on 34 years, and I am now the skipper/owner of my own scallop boat fishing from Meva. In between these years I had the privilege of working with some excellent skippers, one being the renowned Freddie Turner, with whom I worked and played hard, for approximately 15 years. Many a tale could be told about time aboard and onshore in the many ports visited around the country and beyond on the *Britannia IV* and *V*, but that would make a book on its own. Miss you Freddie.

It's lovely to see youngsters in Meva becoming involved in the industry, many owning their own boats, ensuring a good future for the port. Although inherently competitive with one another, fishermen of the village are a strong band of brothers.

To sum up my life as a fisherman: my body tells me different to my mind! The job, particularly in my 20s and 30s kept me away from home for long periods, missing family and children growing up. However, I did get to see and chat (just a little, I promise!) with some great fisher folk, stretching from St. Kilda down to Newlyn, Ireland and France.

JORDAN BALL

APPRENTICE CARPENTER & FISHERMAN

My first experience of fishing was at secondary school. I remember going out with Matt Hunkin on the *Pimpernel* with hand lines catching mackerel at 14 years old. I also remember going out with James Trevarton on his punt. On weekends I would go out with my dad catching scallops on the *Charlotta*, around the coast.

Later, I worked for Jack West on the *Ann Louise* trawling in the winter months. We trawled for cuttle fish or haddock, lemon sole, Dover sole, and Cornish sole (megrim) - until I was airlifted off the boat!

We were on the last day of a four-day trip when a shackle came loose and the next minute I am passed out in the wheel house. Jack called the emergency services and I was tended to on the boat, then airlifted to hospital for a head scan and diagnosed with concussion. It turned out that James and Andrew Trevarton were on their boat fishing nearby and they came to help. James helped Jack get the fish on board too.

It was a freak accident and swiftly dealt with, but it put me off fishing, especially as my son Brody was soon to be born. I re-evaluated my career in fishing. I was so grateful to Jack for his swift action and to the emergency services; but it's a whole different perspective out at sea with an emergency! I then started a carpentry apprenticeship and college course as a new direction and will qualify in September 2022. Now I fish out of Newlyn with Brackan Pearce once in a while.

ROBERT 'TICH' PRESTON

CHAIRMAN OF FISHERMEN'S ASSOCIATION & RETIRED FISHERMAN

I was a part-time Mevagissey fisherman and retained fireman, until I retired in 2006 and then became Chairman of the Fishermen's Association, when Les Hunkin (Skipper) retired. It's a voluntary organisation and I had the time to commit, to take up the fight on various issues. In the early days it was the netting problem in the bay that prevented fishermen from setting nets with a headline below three metres of the surface. The environmental agency disputed it, for the salmon fishermen up the river Fowey, but there were none – it was just if they did! Since then we have had a battle over the mussel bed farms; we had a chap come down from Scotland, because they have salmon farms, who headed 'Crown Estates'. We had a meeting with him, Inshore Fisheries and Conservation Authorities, Harbour Trust and Fowey Sea Farms, and a consultant from Bristol, who put in for the licence. We lost it, because all the fishermen who'd be displaced by the mussel farm going in were all seasonal fishing and not all-year-round fishing, like the farm!

I have attended the meetings for the past five years, representing the 60-plus registered Mevagissey fishing boats for their fishing quotas, with 'South West Quota Advisory Group', that meets in Plymouth about five times a year. Our topic is what should be allocated for the forthcoming months ahead. The quotas have gotten easier over the past twelve months with the availability of fish around. And different fishing affiliations join us in the forum, with usually 18 sat at the meeting

LEE AND DI YOUNG

THE SHIP INN

"Lil is happy as long as she is in the right place, behind the bar"

Lee and Di took over the Ship Inn in January 2013, it was a new venture for them having never worked in pubs previously. The pub's old beams, wooden pillars and ship memorabilia makes it feel homely and warm.

Flooding has always been a continuing problem for the pub as it is the lowest point in the village so is usually affected by the spring tides. "In the summer it is quite entertaining, customers will be sitting there and the pub begins to flood, they don't know whether to stay or go, some just take their shoes and socks off and sit and take pictures. One customer was heard to say on the phone: 'It's like being in a real boat!'

It is a great community; when we have a considerable flood, there are always people who offer to come and help, they put on their flip flops or wellies and wade in. We bale out, bleach through and carry on.

We have a resident ghost in the building who has been seen by quite a few visitors and her presence felt in one of our guest rooms. Her name is Lil and she was landlady in the pub in the early part of the 20th century and died in the 1940s. Her picture hangs behind the bar.

We have many guests who return year after year to stay in the pub as well as many locals who come in regularly. We pride ourselves in using local produce for our meals, we get our scallops from fisherman Brian Ball and buy our fish from the Lakemans, Ocean Fish.

We've had so many characters from the village who would come in, who have sadly passed away who always had great stories to tell."

MEVAGISSEY RETAINED FIRE CREW

"We are similar to the RNLI for fishermen but on land; our firefighters attend Mevagissey harbour and surrounding areas 24 hours of any day to assist in an emergency rescue"

Mevagissey Fire Station is tucked away in a quiet corner of the village, going about its business, usually unseen by the majority of residents. The officers and crew are retained firefighters and live and work within four minutes of the station. The crew essentially are part of the tapestry of life around the port, with varied trades and skills, and are also fully trained and competent fire fighters on call day or night!

Mevagissey was one of the first coastal fire stations to be issued with a marine ejector pump, a piece of equipment that has proved invaluable over the years, pumping out fishing vessels when the need has arisen. It was seen as being such essential equipment in their rescue scenario, it's now standard issue for all fire appliances.

The nature of fishermen's work and the dangers involved will inevitably lead to an emergency call when the fire service's skills are required. The crew trains regularly in practising pumping out drills and ship firefighting skills, both in the station and on scene at the quayside. Harbour Masters and trustees have always supported us in allowing full access onto the quay for the fire crew and emergency services. We are prepared for all eventualities!

MEVAGISSEY COASTGUARDS

"The team is involved in skilled search and rescue on cliffs and/or water, 24 hours a day, working with land, sea and air emergency rescue teams"

Mick Pryor is the Station Officer of Mevagissey coastguard team of 12 volunteers, and we can be tasked to any area. We are notified via our pagers by Falmouth Coastguard Control, which is contacted by the public or the police of an emergency situation requiring our skills, that may also involve the services of the RNLI and Coastguard helicopter, Fire Brigade, Ambulance Service or even Bomb Disposal Unit. The team is on constant standby.

We train every other Thursday and go on courses for first aid, rope rescue techniques and water rescue training; and work closely with St Austell Coastguards with training and rescues in the catchment area, dependent on the type of rescue required and number involved. We even visit schools and local fêtes, to promote safety awareness amongst the community and how to respect the potential dangers of the coast and sea. Needless to say, it's an amazing thing to be involved in a successful rescue as a team.

PAUL PEARCE

ELECTRICIAN

"I'm like a stick of rock: if you snapped me in half, I would have Mevagissey in the middle!"

I was always going to be an electrician. From the age of four I used to love to go to work with Father on a Saturday morning. At this time my dad, John, used to do aerials and need a very tall ladder and he would say, "Look boy you better stay down there" but on one occasion when he was at the top of the ladder on a really tall building, he turned around and I had followed him to the top! Nothing was going to stop me! I knew right through school I was always going to be doing electrics. I was always fiddling around at home with batteries and bulbs and Dad would always encourage me and we would make things together including a fantastic model railway that we built.

I went to college for two years and did electrical and electronic engineering and electrical insulation training with a view that when I finished the course, I would go with Father and we would work together, and in 1986 we did just that. We worked with Dave Churms a lot as he was always building something! We did all the wiring for The Captain's Table project at the end of the harbour. A few years later, my brother Julian joined the business and the three of us worked together and we always got on really well. After ten years, in 2000, Julian moved out of the village and went on to work for an electrical firm in London. He then moved to Helland where he picked up work for local builders.

I love working in Meva, especially around the harbour. I don't like being on the water particularly. I get seasick. I have been known to be wiring some electrics on the boat for Peter Moor alongside the quay and feel seasick just bobbing about! I have been in the Community Fire Service since 1986 and have been station manager for over 20 years. We have a great team and try and do our best for the village and St Austell. It is a massive part of my life. The Mevagissey Choir is also important to our family. My dad, my son and myself are all members. We also as a family spent many years being involved in the St Blazey operatic society for which I am still Chairman.

I love the harbour and everything that goes on in Meva. Why would you want to be anywhere else?

JOHN PEARCE

ELECTRICIAN

"I have worked in Meva now for 37 years on electrics and still am at 85! I love what I do!"

John is a familiar face around the village usually wearing his overalls and woolly hat and a cheeky smile as he sets about his daily work as an electrician, which at the age of 85 is highly commendable.

"I still sing in the Mevagissey Male Choir and have done so since it formed in the 1970s. Paul also sings in it, and now his son Alex has joined. Three generations in one choir! Julian also used to sing in the choir till he moved to Helland where he still lives and works as an electrician. I also play a tea chest bass in a ukelele band which I love, and we go out playing to anyone who wants to hear us, no charge!

I help around the village when I can, and for that I received a Good Citizen Award back in 2008 when I met the St Austell Mayor.

That more or less sums up my life here in lovely Mevagissey!"

MEVAGISSEY MALE CHOIR

Fishing is the history of Mevagissey and the heart and soul of the village. It saw the birth of Mevagissey Male Choir, in Percy Mitchell's boatyard, back in November 1974, when around 20 men from Mevagissey and nearby Portmellon gathered to seek an outlet for their love of singing.

Although sadly, no fishermen sing with the Choir today, our 60 or so members still practise within 200 yards of Mevagissey harbour, perform a series of open-air concerts every summer on the harbour's edge and keenly supporting the village's other traditional events. Our free Monday evening quayside concerts in August draw many hundreds of holidaymakers and locals alike, to the harbour.

As we approach our 50th anniversary, we have considerably broadened our repertoire accordingly with old and new music. Our arrangement of songs from Freddie Mercury, Eric Clapton, Jeff Lynne, Carly Simon and many others, along with our versions of popular classics, such as Bizet and Puccini, have all been warmly received.

With our novel musical approach, we have never forgotten our roots, and regularly mix Cornish and maritime traditional favourites, along with our new arrangements. It was our much loved arrangement of 'Lower Lights' that the Choir performed on BBC's 'Songs of Praise' at Christmas 2018.

Through the years, the Choir has performed over a thousand concerts, travelled to a dozen different countries, sung in the Royal Albert Hall, Westminster Abbey and on board *The World* cruise liner. We are proud that along the way, we have raised many thousands of pounds for a host of charities and good causes, including the Fishermen's Mission and the RNLI.

MEVAGISSEY LADIES CHOIR

"We are very dedicated at our practice evenings and we still manage to have a laugh"

The Mevagissey Ladies Choir was formed in 1985 with 17 members. Two of the founder members still sing with the choir: Angela Blamey and Janet Rowe. The choir has performed concerts for charities including the Air Ambulance, Mount Edgcumbe Hospice, Children's Hospice South West, Mind and the Samaritans, to name just a few. The choir also sings at events such as Mevagissey Feast Week in St Andrew's Church.

One of the highlights of the year is when the Ladies Choir joins the Mevagissey Male Choir, along with the Mevagissey School Choir, to perform a concert at Christmas. The ladies are extremely dedicated and practise weekly at St Andrew's Church. They recognise that having fun is an important part of singing, as well as entertaining their audience.

MIKE AVENT

FISHERMAN

"I have had a wonderful life and would do it all again if I had my time over"

I was born in 1947 and have lived in Mevagissey all my life. My mother's side of the family are the Pollards, a long-standing fishing family and I suppose much of that has rubbed off on me. I left school at 15 and was expected to go into a trade as we all had to do back then. I spent three years serving my apprenticeship with a local builder, and happily packed up in 1966 to begin my fishing career.

That same year the mackerel fishery started and put many young fishermen on their feet, including me. I had a 21-foot boat *Guide Me* built at Looe which I kept for a couple of years, then had the 27-foot *Ocean Queen* built which I fished in for ten very successful years catching mackerel in the winter and crabbing in the summer. In 1979 I had the *Mordros* built which I kept for 33 years. After a couple of years, the shellfish declined a bit so I switched over to monolining for whiting in the summer months which I really enjoyed, as well as netting and longlining. She was a marvellous boat providing a good life for my family and she never let me down.

I have been married to Clare for 40 years and we have two children, Natalie and Tom, who both still live in the village, with our three grandchildren.

Tom, my son, began fishing when he was 16 joining me aboard the *Mordros*. Eventually Tom and I had a couple of bigger boats. Tom is now the owner of the Newlyn trawler *Imogen*. Natalie's partner is the owner of *Kingfisher*, so fishing is still very predominant in our family. I now have an 18-footer which I tinker about in. I have had a wonderful life and would do it all again if I had my time over.

CLARE AVENT

FISHERMAN'S WIFE

"Fishermen are like hunters; they will try and try until it comes good for them"

I met and married Mike when I was 18, and forty years later I can say that life is never dull being married to a fisherman! It's a way of life for you both. You can't plan anything. If you do, things will change; the weather alters course and now the day out you had planned has to wait.

I think it takes a very special type of person to become a fisherman. There can't be many jobs where you go off to work, put in long hours in sometimes terrible conditions, away from your family, with no guarantee that you will end up with a wage at the end of it. I can think of many times over the years when Mike has gone to sea and come in with little or no catch, only to do it all again the following day. But that's how fishing is. Fishermen are like hunters; they will try and try until it comes good for them.

We had two children and I was very lucky I didn't have to go to work. I was able to support Mike by doing his book work. I would drive his fish to Looe fish market four or five times a week, as well as driving to Truro to collect his bait. I was very involved with his fishing life. I look at the younger fishermen's wives today juggling supporting their husbands, bringing up their children as well as many of them working full-time. Life must be hard going for them at times.

Once our children were older, I went to work as secretary for Truro Harbour Master. My colleagues would often ask what I was doing for Easter, or maybe New Year's Eve. They clearly had no idea that fishing doesn't stop for anything; all the days are the same! I can remember one year my family being horrified when Mike was missing on Boxing Day. When I said he had nets to haul they thought I was joking!

I used to worry about him going fishing when he was younger, as he can be rash at times especially as he fished by himself for many years.

In recent years he has bought a couple of cabin cruisers and turned them into fishing boats.

We bought Wild Air Guest House in 1999 which I have run. Due to the coronavirus pandemic Mike has been around a lot more so has lent a helping hand. At 74 he is supposed to be semi-retired, but even now he says fishing comes before hoovering. It's his life and always will be.

TOM AVENT

FISHERMAN

"My love for the sea began when I was four years old"

My love of the sea started at a very early age. At four years old I would go down the harbour with my dad playing around on the boat. As I got older dad taught me to scull the punt; we would shoot a prawn pot or use my dip net. Later I started going fishing at weekends and in the holidays, Dad was always glad of the help as he worked single-handedly. There were also 'school training days' when Mum would agree to it.

When I left school at 16, I went fishing full-time with Dad aboard the *Mordros*. I look back and wonder how I ever stuck at it, with the smell of salted mackerel which we used for bait and when you wanted a cup of tea Dad would fire up the paraffin cooker with methylated spirits; the cocktail of smells would have me instantly throwing up over the rail before we got to Chapel Point!

When I was 18 we bought a scalloper called the *Investor.* A few years later there was an increasing haddock fishery so when I was 24, I bought the trawler *Imogen.* Dad was not so keen so I worked the boat with one crewman. Dad decided to semi-retire and bought a smaller boat.

Finding crew has become more difficult, so last year I decided to diversify and bought a rib, the *Bouncing Betty* which I work in the summer months for coastal speedboat rides for locals and tourists in and around Mevagissey Bay. At present a Newlyn skipper is working Imogen out of Newlyn, and now the summer season has ended, I am working my brother-in-law's trawler the *Kingfisher.*

My wife Ema has supported me through my fishing career. During the summer she pops down to the harbour with my lunch between rides. My daughter Daisy also helps out ensuring everyone has their lifejackets on before climbing aboard. It won't be long before her younger brother Arthur is there as well. A real family affair!

MATT CAVE

SKIPPER OF THE DILIGENCE

"I had tunnel vision to work the sea, the sheer enjoyment of going out fishing, no two days are same"

Mum's side of the family have been here for God knows how long. Dad from London, came down here for a holiday, went home and jacked the job in and came back here.

No other interests in anything – it's fishing or nothing. I could get on the school bus and like couldn't get down quick enough. I had no idea, just had tunnel vision, just the sheer enjoyment of fishing, not the money, nothing the same, all about fish in the boxes. Later as you get older you think of family, you wouldn't care about the amount of fish, just that you had fish. Just the enjoyment of being there, you got the fish through knowledge, whatever but only you did it – the sense of satisfaction. Mevagissey harbour is home, you wouldn't drive me away for nothing.

My wife is Carla, two children Erin (eleven) and Ben (seven). My eldest, two or three times a year will come out with me. Fishing trips summer holidays, mostly mackerel trips, odd angling trip. I get involved every year with the charity angling competitions that raise money for the Fishermen's Mission. It's been going some time. So difficult now for youngsters who can't start until 16/17. Everyone knew their limits, being raised by the village – if anybody did anything, even the slightest thing that went wrong, the parents would soon find out. We were safe as everyone knew us. Not as secure now, as it was when I was growing up. I wouldn't want to live anywhere else. My wife is from Basingstoke area; the quality of our children's lives against theirs of the same age is not comparable.

CHARITY ANGLING DAY – JOHN EDGE

It was started in the 1980s and was first named Shark Fishing Day as a competition for the largest shark caught until sharks became a protected species in the 1990s. So instead of catching sharks we had a sea angling challenge. Six to eight fishing boats would go out for the day with about 40 people. Whoever caught the most fish won but it was mainly about raising money for the charities that the fishermen supported: Fishermen's Mission, Cornwall Hospice and Cornwall Air Ambulance. We would raise £2,500-£3,000 shared between the charities each year.

Gary Tyler is another always involved with the Charity Angling Day – it's a very popular annual event in Mevagissey with sea anglers that the fishermen support with their boats and time.

CHARITY ANGLING DAY – GARY TYLER

"I revived the Charity Angling Day all those years ago; I ran that for ten years or more and we raised £35,000. A third went to the Fishermen's Mission, a third to Cornwall Air Ambulance and a third to the Cornwall Hospice"

John Edge has always done the Mevagissey Charity Angling Day. When I left, John took it on but I am coming back to help with it again. He organised the fishing boat side for a day's sea angling and I organised the activities in the pubs and I would do the pig racing and music and all sorts of activities. Both ventures raised money for the charities. It's a logistical nightmare organising the boats but everyone enjoys it on the day.

It's been going for a great many years and I have trophies dated from the 1960s and I've been involved in it since 1995 but before, what used to happen was; a pub would support a boat each and whoever won the biggest catch on their boat, it was down to the pub to run it for the next year. We even sold cheeky logo T-shirts promoting the day. Then it stopped for a couple years and myself, 'Zippy' and Graham Lawrence decided to form a small committee and to take it on. So that is how it got started again and got mentioned in the top angling magazines and we had a really good following with it. And next year we are hoping to have it even better than before.

JAMES PRYNN

FISHERMAN

"We know the risks and we have the common sense on what weather you can go out on and keeping discipline to get through a lot of it. On your days off there is always work to do on your boat, nets and pots"

I work single-handed fishing during the spring and summer on my boat *Carpe Diem* netting and potting. I started when I left school at 17 years old. Then during the winter months I work as part of a crew on the bigger boat *Galwad-Y-Mor* doing night trips away with Peter and Chris Blamey. I occasionally do a five-day trip away with Peter Blamey in the summer.

We lived and were born in Meva and when we came home from school, we'd go down the harbour and help land the boats and just got into fishing that way. We all naturally grew into fishing and now can't get out of it but not many of the younger generation are coming into fishing at the moment in Meva. There's not much to offer; it's windy, wet, unsocial hours and hard work! But I do like fishing. I hate getting up early in the morning but once I'm up I do like it. I can get up at 3am and be back by 10 or 11am I'm quite independent but you got to be flexible and with a young family now; two little girls ruling the house! It's why I love going fishing!

ASHLEY PARKER

PARTNER OF JAMES PRYNN

Having a fisherman as a partner can be hard in more ways than one. I find myself worrying when James is at sea and feeling relieved when he is back home. It's difficult at times, as there are no set days off and it's not a nine-to-five job. However, we are lucky enough to have a life which suits us all and we enjoy every moment we can all spend together. The money is not guaranteed and the weather is a factor on whether James can fish or not. I suppose with all this in mind it's vital that James gets out fishing when he can. It's a job in itself to fit family life around fishing, but we somehow manage.

It isn't all negative. We have a lovely home in a beautiful part of Cornwall, with an amazing family who love each other. We enjoy our trips out to sea in the summer seeing dolphins up close. It makes me appreciate all the more, the life we have. Yes, the washing of fishing clothes is not the greatest but knowing our children are happy, loved and are lucky enough to grow up near the sea, seems to make it all worthwhile. The supply of fresh seafood is a bonus too. I'll never stop worrying about James. But I can honestly say knowing how hard he works and the effort he puts into fishing, giving us the life we live, makes me ever so proud of the man he is.

Inset: the late Paul Solomon

MALCOLM SOLOMON

FISHERMAN

"There's a few of us here who've been in what's called the 50mph club – pushing weather you shouldn't go out in"

I never did the last two years of school. My father never went fishing but his father did. My father went into engineering as he used to get seasick in the boat in the harbour. My mother died quite early and my father brought us up with my sister and brother.

In the early days, I spent ten days away on a trip, a long time away from home, all those years ago. I'd come in, throw my hat in the porch, very ratty, the kids would look up and say, "Who are you?" Grown up now, I've got two children. Kerry, she lives in Colchester, full-time mother and was a manager at Sainsbury's; she went to Uni and never came home. And my son I now work with, Christopher. He's taken over the family boat, *Likely Lad*.

Sheila, my wife, she works in the kitchen at the Tavern, met her ten years ago, she's from Blisland, Bodmin. Between us now we've eight grandkids. My brother, a well known chap, Paul, died very young. He never quite got where he wanted to get with fishing. A very hard worker but he never got to be a skipper, never quite got there.

My and Mike Brokenshire's claim to fame: marching though St Austell with a gang of fishermen complaining about no sole and no cod and on the dole. It was around '86. It was the start of the cod boats coming in and quotas. We went to every meeting. It was decided that we couldn't catch any more cod and the sole quota was right down on the floor. We decided to march, why St Austell I don't know! We ended up getting shunted into a room away from the dole office and only six of us were allowed in. A protest to the press that we had to sign on, there were fishermen from Mevagissey, Newquay and Padstow. I remember them saying, "Sorry Mr Solomon you can't have the dole, you can't have no cod and you can't have no sole".

CHRIS SOLOMON

SKIPPER OF LIKELY LAD

"The weather this winter has been terrible, the worst we have had for a long time, but come the summer it will all be forgotten"

I have been fishing now for 14 years and my first pay packet was £500, so I never looked back after that good catch. But there are times where it's really hard going. I enjoy being my own boss, going out when I please, unless the boss at home tells me to go out!

We have two girls, four and seven years old, thank God! I would hate to put them in the fishing industry; I'd worry too much for them. It can take you 12 hours to get to where you need to be to catch the fish and no guarantees and weather-dependent. My dad told me he never wanted me to be in the fishing industry, but I was no good in college, and thought it was the only future I could have. So I go out fishing and look forward to coming home to my family. It was easy before we had the children. I didn't worry about going out fishing or the weather. Now I have them, I am total provider and so aware of them.

CLARE AND THE LATE CHRIS ROBINS

"Chris was entrepreneurial and built up different businesses in the village"

I was born in Wimbledon and lived most of my life in the home counties but also in Scotland and for a time in California where I had antique businesses. When lifting and carrying furniture became too much, I went into the paintings market. I also lived in Lymington where I had a similar view to what I have now and owned two antique shops there. When my marriage broke up, I went on to work in the vending trade and it was at a planned meeting with my boss in a pub in Weybridge in Surrey that I met Chris. He was meeting a friend with whom he was arranging a visit to the Hotel Olympia to help choose a wine list for her new restaurant in the town. I ended up sitting on his table and we started chatting while we waited. Then they both turned up together rather the worse for wear. Chris and I spent the evening together, me explaining how I intended to move to Cornwall with my daughter, Natalie. As Chris was very familiar with the county, he agreed to help me and after visiting at half term, I bought a place in Mevagissey. Our love for sport brought us closer together and Chris and I eventually married and he helped me to bring up my daughter. We were together for 31 years.

Chris was always very sporty. He was an Olympic-standard gymnast, achieved a sports degree at university and went on to work at Westminster College in London. Chris's father, Nick and his uncle William ran a fish merchant business. When his uncle died, Chris's father called on Chris to return to Cornwall to help run the business. The Robins had bought an orchard in Mevagissey where, in the pilchard days, they built a salting and packing business. It employed nearly 200 women, nearly all from the village, and exported all over the world. When the pilchards went away, so did the employment and the factory was demolished and turned into a car park, which was known as Sunny Corner. Chris was very entrepreneurial. Not only did he run the car park but he opened a restaurant and seafood bar on the quay with his first wife Roma. His three sons, Conrad, Bevis and Leon were all involved in the running of the business during their upbringing in Mevagissey. Chris grew and supplied all the vegetables for the restaurant. He also built and ran the Cellar Bar which was the only pub with outside space in the village. Chris always cared about the harbour and he was proud to be the chairman of the Harbour Trustees for many years.

When I moved to Mevagissey, Chris taught me the restaurant trade and I worked for a while in the King's Arms. I worked mostly in the car park which I enjoyed. My daughter tragically died very young, which meant due to circumstances, Chris and I then brought up my granddaughter Gwen. She and her partner now have a son of their own.

We sold the car park in 2013. Sadly, Chris developed Alzheimer's and needed full-time care. He passed away in May 2021. I miss him very much.

Recently, I have gone into business with Alex Williams. We have opened a shop where local crafts people can sell their work. It is important for me to support local people and by opening 'Out of the Blue' we hope to do just that.

DON HAWKEN

"I went from being a carpenter to working on engines"

My beloved wife Gillian and I came to Mevagissey in 1969. We moved in with my wife's cousin Frederick 'Peter' Johns and his parents in 10 Polkirt Hill, and I have lived there ever since. Peter was one of the main engineers on the harbour, keeping the thriving fishing fleet at sea. He was one of the cleverest men with his hands you could ever meet. I learnt such a lot from him.

I worked for the china clay industry for much of my life, from 1960, when I finished my apprenticeship, until 1997 when I was made redundant. I then started working with Peter who was the marine engineer in Mevagissey for many years. I went from being a carpenter to working on engines! I also had a part-time job on the harbour. I took money for the car park in the blue hut which is still on the jetty. It was one of the best jobs I had. I met so many different people. I did that for 11 years.

About 40 years ago I made headlines in the local paper for saving the life of a baby boy in the harbour. A car had driven off the edge of the quay. A Royal Marine had dived in to rescue a man and a baby who was on the back seat. I was called out of the workshop and took the baby, who had turned blue and was not breathing and performed CPR on him. He coughed and spluttered, covered me with milk and started breathing! I didn't care; I was so pleased I'd saved his life. I've never heard or seen the family to this day. I was a member of the St John Ambulance (SJA) in Par for 12 years and first aider for ECLP and was congratulated in a letter from the then Commander and Commissioner of the SJA at the time.

During my time in the workshop helping Peter, we fixed everything from Kelvin engines that were in the big boats, to Listers that were in the small boats. Fishermen would even come from other ports to the workshop to pick up spare parts or collect something Peter had repaired that they'd broken! Another job I remember was fixing the ice plant which was going to cost the harbour a lot of money. Peter sat back, put his mind to it and even got that up and running again so the boats could carry on landing their catch in Mevagissey.

Peter and I had a fishing boat, *the Grebe*. It was a tosher built in Portloe. We took it to Gary Mitchell's and we had a foredeck put in and a canopy. Then we added a diesel and a petrol engine. When the weather was fair and we both had a spare evening, we would go fishing with rods on the inshore wrecks. 40st of pollock was a regular event for a short trip angling!

My biggest interest in life is the Great Western Railway. When Freddie Turner's boat, *Britannia V* was being built over 35 years ago, they had different materials left over. We took two pieces of steel from the tanks and we started building the *King George V*, a Great Western Railway engine. It took us 22 years to complete. Every Christmas we would have three weeks off and Peter and I would concentrate on building the model train.

Peter and I made many more models. The last one we did was a four-cylinder engine which was used in the cotton mills in Wigan. All the models that we made were fully working ones. My daughter and grandsons each have one, all of them made in the workshop.

Luke my grandson remembers watching Peter and I busy in the workshop. He said, "One thing I will always remember is the fishermen would often bring something in to be fixed. Peter and Gramps would always do it, often never charge. A favour for a favour and we were never short of fish! Gramps and Uncle Peter also built model railways for Kyle and me."

I now spend much of my time watching over the quay from my window where I can see Kyle my grandson working on his fishing boat entering and leaving the harbour. I sit here reflecting on my life and enjoying my much-loved pipe.

Peter Johns in his workshop

KYLE ROBINSON

FISHERMAN

After spending lots of time growing up in Mevagissey with my grandparents it was clear that all I wanted to do was become a fisherman. Once school had finished I would get picked up by my grandad and taken back to Mevagissey where I'd then be out on the harbour, helping boats land, shovelling ice, moving nets around and I loved it. Weekends I'd be allowed out on the boats (as I didn't have to get up for school the next day) and this is where it all started. I bought myself a small boat.

Once I left school I went to work on a bigger boat in the harbour trawling and scalloping. When I had enough money to buy a bigger boat for myself I did. I then worked that boat full-time netting and handlining. I then got a slightly bigger boat which I work now.

Fishing is a way of life, it's not just about going to sea and coming in again. When I'm not at sea you'll find me rigging new nets or catching up on jobs on the boat as there's always something to do!

GEOFF DANIELS

BUILDER & FISHERMAN

"I was taught by the old boys how to go crabbing"

I grew up in Portmellon and at about nine years of age used to go out with the other kids, fishing off a small punt, and progressed from there. I then had a boat in Gorran where I was taught by the 'old boys' how to go crabbing and where to put the pots and it went from there.

I go fishing part-time as I am a builder. I have a Plymouth Pilot called *Three Boys*, a reliable and seaworthy fishing boat which I can take out in all weathers. It came from Portloe and was named by the fisherman who had three sons. I mainly do crabbing, lining for mackerel, red mullet nets and sole nets. I put the crab pots on from April onwards and pull them out at Christmas time when the shellfish go out to the deeper waters.

Everyone says I go out fishing in too rough a weather but I love it and I have a boat that can cope with it!

ANDY SHAW

SKIPPER OF THE DEFIANT

"Offered a job, thought it would be a six-month working holiday; basically I never went back"

I left school in 1977 and have been fishing ever since. I grew up in the North East and fishing was always in the family, more so on my mother's side. Her family name was Lince, a well-known fishing name. My mother and father live up in Redcar and I try and get up to see them but Mevagissey is home.

As a younger fisherman I remember staying in the rooms of the old Fishermen's Mission centre in Hull, where we'd billeted down for the night in between fishing trips. I'd deep-sea fish out of Hull, then I moved to inshore fishing around Whitby and Redcar until I moved down to Mevagissey in 1980/81. I was offered a job, thought it would be a six-month working holiday; basically I never went back.

For the last 18 years I've skippered the trawler, *Defiant*. It's owned by a Plymouth company Victory Fishing but I work it out of Mevagissey. Bradley Collings has been with me for the last five years, I work it with one crew, before that Tim Blamey and then it was with some of the lads from Newlyn. Always been lucky to have a steady crew, treat them as you expect to be treated yourself. I've a son, Nathan, and daughter Jenna.

ROB HIGGENS

FISHERMAN, ELECTRICIAN & COMPUTER SYSTEMS ENGINEER

"It all started when I moved to Mevagissey because I was under such pressure from my business; I'd built a call centre in Ashford and nearly had a heart attack from the stress! I was on call, literally attached to a phone 24/7 as I was totally responsible for its running. I moved here giving remote support until I cut the contract with them. I stepped onto the fishing boat for the first time and there was literally no contact with them!"

I was able to get grants to acquire my 'tickets' for the qualifications to go to sea as a crew member on Chunky's boat (John Hunkin). I always took my tool kit with me and was often fixing things as they broke; it was good to repair out at sea rather than having to come back. Me and Chunky share a punt between us, so I service it and go out on my own for headspace.

I'm a qualified electrician and have a computer systems engineering degree and because of this background I can step on a boat and cover all fields of repair for the radar, sonar and electrical equipment. My qualifications allow me to do all the 'grunt work' instead of sending up-country to get it fixed for them. Last year I completely refitted Chunky's boat over two months; it took three miles of cable alone! In a house you have one voltage, on a boat you have five and have to be careful amongst the oil and watery bowels of a boat.

DAVID BOWMAN

MEVAGISSEY SHARK ANGLING CENTRE

"What a view every day, there's always something different"

Originally from Nottingham, Dave and his wife Elaine spent many wonderful holidays in Cornwall with their family. In Nottingham, Dave was a project engineer but they followed their dream to come to Cornwall and opened a business in Mevagissey.

"We were in Portmellon and my son wanted to go mackerel fishing on one of the four-hour trips, so we came into Mevagissey. That was when I saw the advertisement in the corner of the shop door: 'Shop for sale'. That was in 1990, nearly thirty years ago! Elaine and I moved down and took over the shop. In the winter I used to go out mackerel fishing with Martin on *Aquila*. Sadly, Elaine passed away in 2003 so I run the shop alone now, although my son Chris comes down when he can, to help out. What a view every day, out over there." He points out to the harbour. "Even when it is raining, you'll always see something different, fishermen will be working on their boats in all weathers. It has been good fun running the shop."

Dave's only regret is that Elaine hasn't been able to share the last sixteen years with him.

GARY FARR

WEST WALL HARBOUR & VALLEY ROAD PUBLIC TOILETS

"As far as the fishing folk are concerned, we provide the toilets free of charge to the fishermen, engineers, harbour workers, or drivers picking up a fish delivery. We gain them access and they don't have to find coins. We try and support them and the locals, as they are paying their rates towards these conveniences"

We are a management company who gained the yearly tender for servicing and maintaining the public conveniences on West Quay and Valley Road on behalf of the Parish Council. I very conveniently live across the other side of the harbour. We maintain every aspect of the public building and services provided attributed to the contract with the Parish Council.

Amenities on the harbour are vital not only to the public but the fishermen and services connected to them who require this facility. The running costs are huge and we need to charge the public a tariff towards this cost. Our interaction with the fishing folk is limited other than fishermen landing who are desperate for the loo; we are happy to give them access.

Going home from work and finding a bag of crab claws on my door handle is a lovely thank-you from an anonymous fisherman. So we know we are appreciated by the fishing folk.

Andrew is the attendant and cleaner all year and Stuart and I do the maintenance work to keep them and other businesses up and running.

From left: Gaynor Walker, Amanda Young, Lesley Dent

AQUARIUM

CURATOR: CHRIS GILBERTSON. STAFF TEAM: AMANDA YOUNG, BEN ROBERTS, GAYNOR WALKER, LESLEY DENT, PAULA SAUNDERS.

"The Aquarium attracts over 100,000 visitors a year"

The Marine Aquarium is situated in the former RNLI lifeboat station and opened in the mid 1950s. In the late 1960s the Harbour Trustees took over the running of the Aquarium and nine years ago it was refurbished using a lottery grant. Opening from Easter to the end of October, it has an average of 100,000 visitors a year and relies purely on donations. It is an independent charity and is listed as an education venue. All the exhibits are supplied by local skippers. The video in the Aquarium, narrated by the former Harbour Master, Hugh Bowles, tells the story of the pilchard industry from the early days when they were exported to Italy in wooden barrels, right through to modern-day fishing where the ring netters catch the fish and do the processing and exporting directly themselves.

There are five staff who work in the Aquarium on a rotation basis. They are there to answer questions and chat about our local species. Both present and past staff who have worked in the Aquarium often have funny tales to share, such as the time someone dropped their glasses into the open tank and the staff member had to recover them amidst the large crabs, lobsters and fish swimming around! Or the time when someone asked if dogs were allowed in and was given the answer, "Sorry no dogs in here apart from dogfish!"

All agree that watching the children's excited faces squashed up against the glass tanks, fascinated by all the different kinds of marine life, makes the job worthwhile.

From left: Steph Dudley, Caroline Varcoe, Susan Edwards

CAROLINE VARCOE

MEVAGISSEY HARBOUR SWIMMERS

"It's nice to have a bit of company swimming, apart from the seal that swims in the harbour; he's pretty big and scary! We love the wash from the boats coming in. We say we are riding the surf!"

It's a good feeling to go cold-water swimming. It releases endorphins and I swim all year around, weather permitting, but I go in every day if I can. I only live around the corner, Susu lives in a flat in the Sharksfin and Stephanie lives up the hill and has been swimming for years. The secret is to not stop swimming; keep going every day, even if you just stand in the water to acclimatise to the cold. I like to go off near the aquarium because it's not in the way of any boats, in my thermal hat and bathers.

As a little girl, my father had a grocery shop next to the old post office in the square. I used to go off with my bathers and a towel to Sandy Beach. There was always a big crowd of mums with their kids on the beach and all would watch out for each other. I learnt to swim on Sandy Beach. I could go back and forward to the shop with no trouble. Only day we didn't go swimming as a child was Sunday, because we'd go to chapel dressed in our Sunday best. It was a safe place to grow up as a child.

MARLENE BEHENNAH

RETIRED MEVAGISSEY GP

"Achieving a good reputation as a GP with the fishermen in the harbour was important"

Marlene and Lynne were both born in Mevagissey. "We were from a fishing family but unfortunately our father couldn't become a fisherman as he was always very sick on boats so they had to tie him to the mast!

I went to Mevagissey School, then the grammar school and was the first person from Mevagissey to go to Oxford University where I studied medicine. A doctor who was a practising GP in the village at the time persuaded me to become a GP myself and there began my career in the village surgery where I stayed for 30 years. When I left university, I returned home as Dr Behennah and on entering the village saw banners up which read, "Well done Mevagissey congratulates you". I thought they were for me but soon realised they were for Jonathan Barron who had just won the amateur snooker championship! That put me in my place!

Bill Hanan, Andrew Crawshaw and I believed in care 'Cradle to Grave.' Together we built a new surgery in the village. It was important to us that it was part of our community. I do remember when I was new to the job of GP, Dr Hanan asked me to do an evening surgery as he was going on holiday. A local fisherman came in with a very loud voice; in his leg he had the biggest conger eel hook you had ever seen! I knew very little about fish hooks and although I did know the procedure to remove it, this was a first. I also knew if I made a mistake my reputation around the harbour would spread very quickly! The pliers I needed to carry out the operation were too small so I sent the receptionist for some larger pliers from the electrician nearby. When he arrived, he admitted he was not good at the sight of blood, so with him looking away and me giving the instructions the hook was finally removed. My reputation was intact!

When I retired 20 years ago, one of my hobbies was to learn Ancient Greek, something which had interested me when I was at university. I have almost translated the whole of Homer!"

LYNNE BEHENNAH

RETIRED PSYCHIATRIST

"Our family has always been obsessed with Christmas"

"Like my sister, Marlene, I went to Mevagissey School and then the grammar school. I always remember Friday afternoons we used to make up plays which I enjoyed. I took part in pantomimes written by Mr Moss in the village who used to change the words of traditional songs to go with whatever play we were doing. I actually wanted to be an actress but unfortunately my teacher told me I wasn't good enough. So, then I concentrated on the sciences and went on to study medicine at medical school. I became a rehabilitation psychiatrist and worked in a hospital in Plymouth. I retired early from the NHS and returned to live with Marlene in Mevagissey."

Although Lynne didn't follow her dream to become an actress, she fondly remembers taking part in the Wildworks presentation of WWI aptly named 'The Day the World Changed': an incredible production which included professional actors and local people performing together, starting at the harbour where Lynne's role was Mayor of Mevagissey, to Heligan where she played the hospital matron and then a farm girl picking turnips in the field all in one day.

"Both Marlene and I love Christmas. When I retired, I decided to set up a small Christmas shop which I ran from a hut in Heligan. I would go to Harrogate to buy stock as well as sell ornaments and decorations made by local people." Although Lynne gave that up several years ago both Marlene and Lynne always make Christmas very special in the village. Their house is full of beautifully decorated trees, one in nearly every room! Often, they have opened their house up to local people to come and admire the decorations as well as the 70 Nativity scenes that Marlene has collected from different countries around the world. Over the last eight years she has organised a Christmas Tree Festival in the Jubilee Hall which has taken place on alternate years. Each business or organisation decorate a tree in the given theme and the public votes for the winner. Crafts and Christmas goodies are sold. All the money raised at these events is given to local charities or organisations.

The local community is very important to both Lynne and Marlene and particularly at Christmas when they enjoy seeing the joy that the different events bring to the people of Mevagissey.

LIZ HURLEY

HURLEY BOOK SHOP OWNER & AUTHOR

Hurley Books is almost twenty years old; it was the best thing we have ever done. Back then I ran the shop and Steve ran the warehouse. Now Emma Hunkin, a Mevagissey girl, runs the shop, while I write and Steve works behind the scenes.

It had been left empty for a while and required gutting. We took the floor up and underneath were cobbles on top of sand and behind the walls were holes for the pilchard presses. So we dry-lined the wall to preserve the history of the lovely old building originally built for the fishing industry.

We opened our shop in December. By 4.30pm it was dark; outside were children playing tag, ducking down the alleyways and doorways. To see children playing like this, I thought they were having a wonderful childhood growing up in such a special place. Unlike a lot of picturesque villages in Cornwall, Mevagissey is still home to many families that have lived here for centuries. We have a Victorian postcard of a group of children staring into the camera on the steps of one of the cottages. On the back someone wrote their names: Barron, Behenna, Hopkins, Hawkins and Robins. The fishing industry has secured the people to the village and so both survived.

I also love it when some of the fishermen would come in with swaps; fish for books that suited me down to the ground. The sheer pleasure of eating lobster for lunch, out on the harbour wall! What a life? Hurley Books continues to flourish within the village.

MARK AND HAZEL CROOK

SALAMANDER RESTAURANT

"We are proud to say we buy our produce locally"

We came to Mevagissey in 2007. We had been looking all over Cornwall from Bude to St Ives, from pubs to cafés and restaurants and then we walked in here and we knew it was the right place. We took over on the Monday and opened on the Wednesday: it was our first business so quite a challenge! I was in catering in the RAF for 12 years and cooking to different standards depending on the posting. I even cooked for the then Prime Minister, Margaret Thatcher, and Russian President Gorbachev! After leaving the RAF, I spent two years in the prison service before cooking in a pub in Yorkshire whilst searching for our own business.

I met Hazel in 1994 when she was managing front of house and bar in an Officers' Mess, having prepared functions during that time for HRH Queen Elizabeth II and other dignitaries. We married in 1996. And now here we are, this is Mevagissey and you don't need to say anymore. All the food we cook in our restaurant is fresh, nothing is frozen. I bake my own bread every day at high season. We buy the smaller, more unusual cheeses which are made locally in individual dairies; we have a man who goes round to these businesses, picks them up and then delivers to us. It's a way of supporting those individual dairies. We buy local meat from Lobbs Farm and also Kendall's at Bodrugan or the farm in Gorran. Strawberries come from up the hill at Boddington's. Our fish is bought from Celtic Fish and Game at St Ives and we buy scallops from a fisherman in the bay. It's great to be able to tell our customers it is all local produce.

We have a tradition that every evening before opening we walk out along the quay. We've been referred to as the loving couple as we are always holding hands! It is always different every day when we look out at the sea, an ever-changing landscape.

TIM BLAMEY

RETIRED FISHERMAN

"Spent all my life fishing. I was working on the fishing boats before I went to primary school. My father fished, grandfather, great-grandfather – I don't know how far we go back fishing"

I have had to retire due to bad health and selling my boat this week and will retire from fishing. Fishing has definitely changed over the years. Nets are made of nylon these days but way back were made of cotton and took a lot of maintenance. Father had our boat built in the 70s and it couldn't be launched until it was named, as it was bad luck. Mother and Father were driving out over Bodmin Moor and drove through a little place called Demelza, and mother said, "There you are there is a Cornish name for your boat", and that was how the boat got named.

Mevagissey harbour has changed so much now. You could see 15 fishermen huddled together talking on one side and the same on the other side. Now they jump in their cars and they are gone!

Eating was the most important thing on the boat and fishing was second. You need to feed your crew well to do the job. If you were out with a 'picky' crew member it made the job hard. All the preparation for going to sea for a week, you can't pop out to the shops! You can't eat the same old thing each day either. Now I think I might keep myself busy setting or making nets, or get a little boat for lobster pots.

JOHN HOCKING

RETIRED FISHERMAN

There's an East side and West side in Mevagissey, the jetty being the middle. West side fishermen would line up on their wall to look out to sea and the East side did similar. When I left school at 16, I stood to line up on the East side and I was told "Get over to your own bloody side".

Around 1954 I was fishing with my father; it was on my great-grandfather's sailing schooner the *Carazel*. It was in the early hours of the morning, the weather was rough and it was raining. I was below deck making a cup of tea when I was asked to keep an eye open. Just on my way up, we grounded ashore at Dodman. I kicked my boots off as I jumped into the water. Reaching the shore with my father beside me, I pulled him up the cliffs. Once at the top, we walked to a farm house. I was walking barefoot through the brambles. The farmer drove us home. We had a new boat built called *Little Fisher* and we were back fishing in the June.

In Mevagissey there were three fish buyers, the Pawlyns, Edwards and Robins. Pawlyn was known as the Big White Chief of Cornwall; what he said, went. He would get one of his workers to go round to the Edwards and Robins on a Friday and tell them what price the fish would be bought for: everyone was paid the same for their fish!

Sheila my wife, was on the local Cancer Research committee. She won an award for raising the most amount of donations just before she was ill. I lost Sheila to cancer just as I retired. A friend asked if I could help him on his boat so I went back to sea and finally retired at 82. I've enjoyed my life. Fishing is a good life. I worked any day and time, not like being in an office. I have two daughters Sarah and Kate, and four grandchildren, two boys of each girl.

MORLEY WESCOMBE RIP

ARTIST & MUSICIAN

"Morley was often asked by visitors while he was sat on the shop window, 'Are you local?' Morley would reply, 'Only when I am at home'"

Morley Wescombe lived above his art gallery at 28 Church St. He was often seen in the shop window painting maritime seascapes or showing another craftsmanship, such as figurehead carving. One particular pair of figureheads can be found aboard the QE2 ocean liner, situated at the bottom of a grand staircase leading to the restaurant.

Morley was also very popular as an entertainer around the village, playing piano in the Fountain Inn and famously at the Harbour Lights on Sundays for Jazz with the 'Clay City Stompers'. Morley was a true village character and was often seen on the harbour doing pen and ink drawings of the harbour. He made a series of postcards of Mevagissey which he sold in his shop to visitors. He was a true Cornishman that sailed the world in the Royal Navy, and father of six children. Many live recordings of Morley's jazz years are found online. He sold oil paintings far and wide. Sadly, since this book went into press, we lost this Proper Job character.

RICHARD WESCOMBE

NET RIGGER & EX-FISHERMAN

"I work just above the Fish Quay; there's a rigging loft up there. I put my radio on and hear the boats coming and going; sometimes I'd nip down the stairs there to see if there was any fish going"

I left home for the bright lights of London when I was younger and then thought "Why did I go away in the first place?" So I came back to the village and was working around the harbour and helping John and Peter Moor in their boatyard. Ted Luck taught me how to bend timbers by steaming them to make replacement ribs for William Shugg's boat *Radjel*.

I fished with Trevor Mannel on the *Vesper* and another boat the *Mary Ann* and on *Radjel* Willy Shugg's boat. That's how I met Brent Young, who was rigging nets for John Hunkin's boat *Celtic Dawn*; he said he had had enough of that, so he gave me lessons and I learnt it off him.

William Shugg was a great help to me, he taught me to gurdy for mackerel and they needed someone to make up the nets so they can get out fishing. It was great to learn how to do it but it's a dying art; there's not many people left who know how to do it. I'll have to find someone else soon to teach how to rig nets to keep it going. It's a nice little job doing the nets for John Hunkin (Chunky).

MICHAEL THOMAS

LANDSCAPER & FISHERMAN

I was out on a boat as soon as I could walk with my dad and grandad. My earliest memory is going out around St Austell Bay with hour-trippers for mackerel, helping people on the slipway. I had a lot of angling trips on the wrecks with my grandad. I used to steer the boat back into harbour, pull up the anchor and help people on the slipway. When he was commercial fishing, I'd have a box of small mackerel and take them to the quay to sell for bait.

Had my first dinghy at nine years old; at 14 years old I bought a punt the *Harlequin* to fish in the evening after school and catch a few mackerel. A few years ago I bought a commercial licensed boat called *Louella*, until due to ill-health I couldn't go fishing alone anymore. So I went out with James Prynn on his boat occasionally but now started a new career pathway.

Blake my lad, I want to give the same happy experiences as I had growing up. I got him a boat to play with in the garden, ropes and crab pots. I got us both some automatic lifejackets and he came out on *Louella* with me. He'd sit up front watching me handlining for mackerel; he'd be fascinated watching them all flapping shinily on the deck. Whether he will go down and do harbour jumping and swimming as I did as a child, I don't know.

MARK THOMAS

RETIRED PART-TIME FISHERMAN

"Me and my boy Michael would go out on the boat mackerelling when he was four or five years old. He'd be curled up in the wheelhouse fast asleep in the warm or out helping me put out the lines, just as I had as a boy"

I remember standing on a fuel tank steering the boat to look out the wheelhouse window to see where I was going, loving every minute of it. I loved being out at sea with my boy, just as my father had when I was a nipper. My father was Ernie Thomas and he retired in 2006 from fishing. He was my best friend and we did commercial and chartered trips from Mevagissey. I got my licences to do both at the age of 17.

Me and my dad caught scallops on the boat *Bunowen II*. We went over to France and bought her in April 1980; a few fishing boats were brought over from France and converted. There was a 'Cooperative' in the 60s that'd pick up the fish from the boats, boxed in ice, and run them to market. Lots of the squid got sent off to Japan! We came in to Mevagissey high or low tide because of the two harbours and the winches; we were fortunate.

There are so many memories of my life at sea, I could fill a book. In my father's day fishermen could tell you what fish were around by what sea birds they saw or the gorse in full flower. Many a time the weather would turn bad; if you got a call for help at sea, you'd go!

DAVID WARWICK

FISHING GEAR INNOVATION TECHNOLOGIST & EX-FISHERMAN

"My dad was a fisherman and I worked with him since I was knee-high. I could never imagine doing anything else — I loved it"

I was a fisherman for 31 years and skipper of the boat *Valhalla*. I have had three boats; all named *Valhalla*. I always said that if I had a boat I'd name it that. It means 'vacant heaven'. I could never imagine doing any other job; I am just attracted to it, maybe in my genes I suppose. We worked together for a number of years, even built a boat together until Dad retired. Then I got my own boat.

Last November I started my new job working as a civil servant, now as a gear technologist. It involves working and helping the fishermen with their fishing gear for optimum catches and giving them advice. Not just Cornish fishermen; wherever they might need my help. We run courses over in Denmark in the 'flume tank': like a large swimming pool with windows in the side and conveyor belt on the bottom and you can see how the trawl behaves under water. It's really interesting and came along at a time where I considered a change from fishing, but I'm still involved and I can give something back to fishing still. It's a home-based job that involves a fair bit of travel.

As yet I have not been missing my fishing because the weather has been terrible, but come the summer, I know I will miss it and will get a small boat. If I had my time again, I would do fishing all over again; I have absolutely loved it. If my son (who is eight years old) wanted to go into fishing, I would support him, but equally I would support him in anything he wanted to do.

JEREMY BLACKMORE

FISHERMAN & OWNER OF THE FISH GRILL

I was over 30 years gill netting, tangle netting and handlining and was in a working partnership for the last 24 years with Andrew Trevarton, the last seven as joint owners of the *Galatea* FY97, a trawler. Trawling wasn't for me so I went part-time for the last few years. *Galatea* is now sold and Andrew has taken the position as Mevagissey Harbour Master while I have now purchased a Kingfisher 20 to carry on netting and handlining; she was originally called *Cormoran* PZ4 but is now called *Midnight* SE9. I have a catering trailer on the harbour during the summer months called 'The Fish Grill' which sells a variety of cooked local fish species and specifically mackerel and sardine fillets, scallops and other fish such as whiting and hake when available. I am passionate about promoting local fish and the fishing industry as a whole. Nothing makes me happier than seeing people enjoying the various fish meals cooked for them. I try to encourage the children to sample the boneless mackerel fillets as it is a delicious healthy tasty option. The boat and 'The Fish Grill' will work well together and allow me to enjoy what I love doing the most; fishing is my way of life and I know I am lucky to be able to earn a living doing this.

MARK GROOM

STREET CLEANER OF MEVAGISSEY

"To me Mevagissey is my home and heaven"

Mark has been in Mevagissey for 18 years. Originally he came from West Bromwich in the Midlands, where he was a self-employed landscaper, working on private estates and gardens. His love for the environment is probably why he treats Mevagissey with as much care as he would his own garden and property. He is far more than his professional title. As well as carrying out his job for the Council, he can be seen around the village maintaining flowerbeds, painting cottages and even on his day off ensuring our village is clean and tidy. He takes great pride indeed in his work!

Mark has many funny tales to relate about situations he has come across in Meva. "I remember a Sunday morning, following Feast Week Saturday, it was about 5.15 and I was tidying up in the street. I came across a young man lying outside the Ship Inn, rather worse for wear. Although he was asleep, I put him in the recovery position safely off the road. A walker with a rucksack went by quite concerned about the chap. I told him not to worry as he would be awake by 6.10. A bit confused he asked how I knew the precise time. I told him the watering system started up then which watered the hanging baskets. Sure enough, that was what happened. The young man woke up soaked and staggered off into the distance!"

In 2017, Mark was nominated by the local councillor for Biffa National Employee of the Month and he duly won the award. More recently, the chairman of Cornwall Council surprised Mark with a Chairman's Gonk Award and a Cornwall Council Good Citizen award for his years of service going above and beyond for the village. Despite the recognition, he remains modest about his achievements and is a well-respected member of the community.

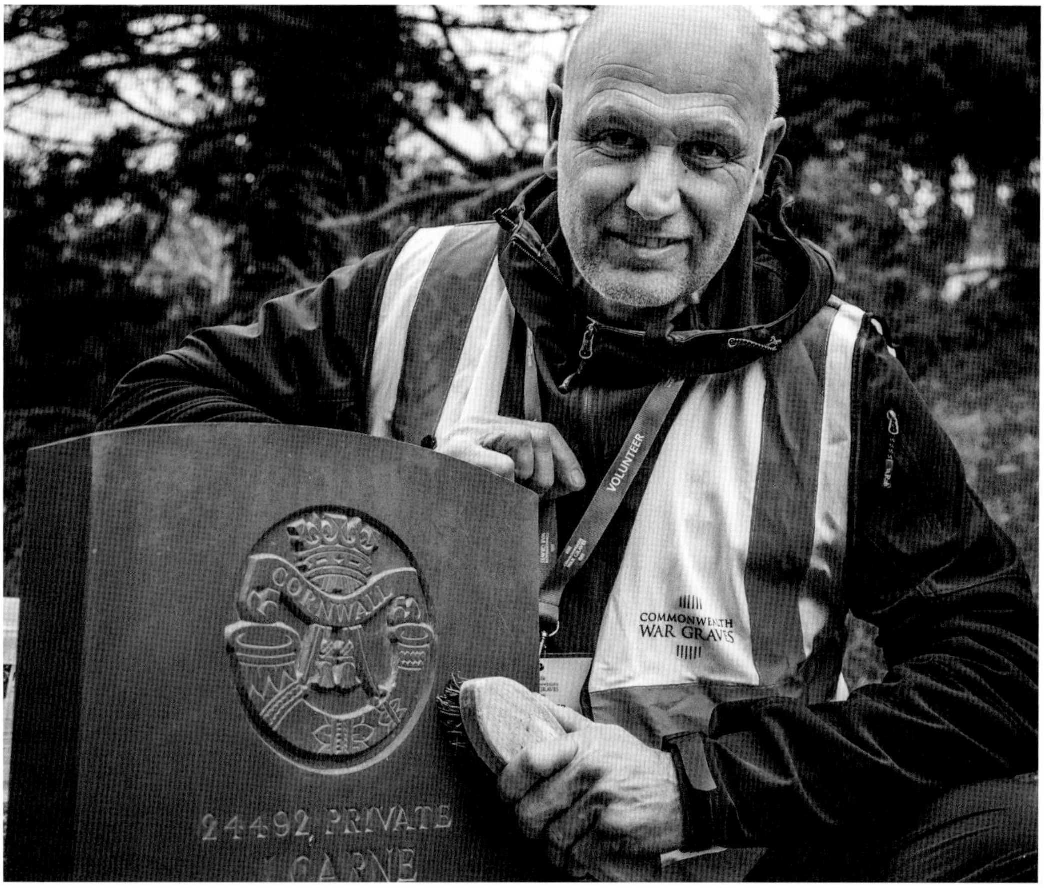

KEV BRADDOCK

COMMONWEALTH WAR GRAVES COMMISSION 'EYES ON, HANDS ON' PROJECT VOLUNTEER

"I've always had an interest. My grandfather was in WWII and was blown up in North Africa, and received serious injuries. He went back down the mines with just one arm, blind in one eye and deaf in one ear! I was walking around our old cemetery in Mevagissey and went to the war memorial, took all the names and realised one of the names from the cemetery wasn't on the memorial"

I researched the name; 'able seaman Ronald Allenby Crunden' who was 20 years old and discovered that his body had been washed up near to Mevagissey. His ship (HMS *Acheron*) had been sunk near the Isle of Wight. They had been doing speed trials in high seas and darkness and hit a mine that had been dropped by the Luftwaffe. The ship went down quickly and nearly all on board drowned.

The research uncovered that his relatives thought he was buried in Eastbourne, where he came from; there was a serviceman with the same initials, surname and age who'd died within months of him. I notified the family in 2019 of the correct grave site, as they weren't aware of it; he also had three brothers, two of whom died in WWII. I gave the family all the details from my research. I researched all the names on the Mevagissey War Memorial for the 100th re-dedication service of the Memorial. I included the information on Ronald, all of which research can be viewed on Mevagissey Museum's website.

MALCOLM 'TRIGGSY' TRIGGS

"Mevagissey is my home. I feel I have never left, just been away now and then"

I was born in Mevagissey to a family who all had links to the fishing industry. My father drove the fish lorry for Pawlyn's. I would often go with him on Saturdays in the 50s and 60s down to the fish market in Newlyn and in the summer holidays up to Billingsgate Market in London. Mum was a Mevagissey maid. My grandad 'Silent Sid' Husband and great-grandad Joe Husband were fishermen. Grandad had a Mevagissey tosher called *Sea Queen* which was the first tosher built by Percy Mitchell in 1924 up the backlet in a workshop before moving to Portmellon. In July 2019 Gary Mitchell (Percy's son) and myself were invited to the Maritime Museum in Falmouth for the launch of *Sea Queen* after she had been restored in workshops at the Museum where she is now a floating exhibit. My great-grandad and grandad had a Cornish lugger called the *Westward* built which was one of the first made by Percy Mitchell in Portmellon in 1925. Unlike my father, grandad, and great-grandad, I did not enter the fishing industry. I was more interested in sport and as a young lad played rugby for English Schools then made the step up to playing senior rugby in 1970 for Penryn and Cornwall.

I moved to South Wales in the early seventies with my work as a GPO /BT engineer. I played rugby in Wales coming home to play for Cornwall in the County Championship. Over the last 25-30 years my work in the telecom industry took us overseas, but we always kept a family home in Mevagissey. Now retired we live permanently in the village. Wherever my wife Sue and I lived, we would always hold a Cornish pasty dinner party, even being able to source turnip, although it was white.

We would always come home wherever we were in the world and never miss Mevagissey Feast Week. I am proud to carry on the fish auction on Fish Sunday in memory of my dear friend, Pete 'the Fish' Randall. Feast Week will always be my memory of Robin Hunkin. When I stand at the top of Hitler's Walk and look over the harbour, the village and up to Heligan House there is no better view in the world.

I am a proud Cornishman; Mevagissey has always been my home and even though I have been away I feel that I have never left, just been away now and then.

THE SHARKSFIN

MELISSA MARQUIS & THE TEAM FROM THE SHARKSFIN AND POLLOCKS PUBS

"The tapestry of what our restaurant is remains entwined with love of seafood and respect for the sea"

Mevagissey was born and raised fishing and what is now the Sharksfin played a significant part in this rich legacy operating in its early years as a pilchard press. The oil from the press would run down the length of our flooring and be collected to sell as lamp oil so if you're standing in our Upper Deck dining area you'll see that the floor tips downwards at a slight angle towards the door.

The tapestry of what our restaurant is remains entwined with love of seafood and respect for the sea and we support the Cornish fishing industry through our menus.

Another strong positive of living in this beautiful village is its genuine community spirit. We love being one of the hubs where locals drop in throughout the day to catch up over a coffee or a meal or a cold beer at the end of the day.

FRANCES & NORMAN THOMAS

"Granfer and Gran would have terrible rows and she'd call him a 'bloody old Spaniard'"

Frances and Norman now live nearer to their adult children in South Wales. There's Stuart, Pip, Lucy and Rachael. Norman's grandparents were Welsh speakers from South Wales and Cornish on the other side from St Germans. Frances' family dates back to the 1500s in Mevagissey. All of their adult children say that they are 'true Celts' with Welsh and Cornish blood.

Frances' family was around at the time of the Spanish Armada. Mevagissey folk were told that if any Spaniard were to be washed ashore alive, they must either be clubbed to death or handed over to militia. A little boy was washed ashore, who'd been in the crow's nest of a Spanish boat, The locals didn't want to turn him in as he was so little, so he was reared in Mevagissey. He was known as Pedro the Moor and that's how Frances' family name Moore derived. This family oral story was passed down through the generations. The eldest boy in the family was always called Peter Moore. Frances remembers Granfer and Gran having terrible rows and she'd call him a "bloody old Spaniard".

Old Mevagissey is still very much in the family's heart, with memories such as attending the Prickly Back Methodist Chapel, now flats.

ROB GREENAWAY

PARAMEDIC & OWNER OF PLEASURE BOAT, SEASCAN

"The harbour – it's my roots. I love being down there"

Rob came to Mevagissey at three days old. His parents then owned Shearwater, a bed and breakfast which was situated at the top of Polkirt Hill, one of the few original houses remaining there. He spoke fondly of his childhood spent in the village.

"At ten years old, my mother introduced me to the fisherman, Spencer Blamey, who would take me down to the harbour where I would do odd jobs on boats and help the fisherman pack the fish." Rob also enjoyed going down to Mitchell's boatyard in Portmellon where he remembers seeing the craftsmen at work, and the smell of the freshly-planed wood used to build the boats remains fondly in his memory.

"At 17, I joined the RAF and worked in London, Scotland and Hong Kong. In 1991 I returned to Cornwall and joined the Cornwall Ambulance Service and trained to be a paramedic, and now work two days a week in Newquay. I continued to fish part-time and have owned several boats over the years. For the last five years I have owned *Seascan*, an ex-trawler which I have converted to carry people during the holiday season. During the last three years a German film company has used *Seascan* to film parts of the films based on the books by Rosamunde Pilcher, which has been interesting.

I think an ex-fisherman who has travelled the world sums up the village very well: 'When the sun is out there is no place like Mevagissey'". A sentiment that Rob shares.

SIMON DUNN

FISHERMAN OF THE DUNN FISHING FAMILY

I was born in 9 Battery Terrace, in the same room my father had been born. Then there were probably 50 Dunns living in the village: now only one is left. I have five children and due to the cost of housing, not one is able to live in the village.

For two years I worked with Geoff and Tommy Blamey, mainly gill netting and feathering, trawling and scalloping, but found on the bigger boats I got quite seasick and felt miserable in bad weather. My grandfather was desperate for me to go fishing. He offered to buy me the biggest boat in the harbour if I went to sea school and got my skipper's ticket. I broke his heart because of my sea sickness – anything seemed better. I'm fine on the smaller boats but this was the 40-60 footers.

My grandparents raised my brother (Ken) and myself from the ages of four and five years old and grandfather (Alf Dunn) was a passionate fisherman. Because grandmother hated it so much, he decided to pursue other business interests. We had three boats in the village. Bill Hocking ran his 25-foot commercial boat Little Nell and two 18-foot boats that we as boys would fish around the bay. I spent a couple of years fishing after leaving school and then joined the armed forces.

I returned three years ago, thinking it was going to be wonderful, when the draw of the sea became strong. The only way I could have a boat in the harbour was to go commercial because you'd get a mooring, so I bought a 21-foot boat. I was able to get a private mooring the following year, so now I can go out when I want to and not because I have to.

My family dates back to the 1600s and most from fishing lineage, but for Captain James Dunn who was a prolific smuggler. His exploits included being captured whilst smuggling during the Napoleonic War. There was a 'Dunn Boat Yard' in Portmellon (car park now) building many boats up to 120-foot sloops. They would build the boats and when it came to launch, the yard went across what is now the road and extended on stilts out on to the beach. I have a list of the boats the Captain built, and approximately 75% were broken up by the Customs and Excise when caught smuggling across from France. He was called 'The Old Reprobate'. He had an office where the old pilchard grill used to be on Fore Street and in the floor is a large glass panel where the tunnels go in under the houses and shops that brought the contraband. He was the main instigator of smuggling in the village and divided out the goods to everyone: preacher, policeman, villagers. Those offices were the hub of the smuggling activity.

So that's my great-grandfather four times removed. His father was also called Captain James Dunn, who sadly died in the cholera epidemic in the 1800s.

When John Wesley came to Mevagissey to preach Methodism for the first time, James and his drunken cohorts went to ridicule Wesley where Trewinney Cemetery is now. John Wesley was brave to return the following year and James listened to him and ended up going around the world with Wesley, and became a Methodist Minister. When Truro Cathedral was built it was multi-denominational and the first stained glass window on the right side is dedicated by John Wesley to the memory of Captain James Dunn and his son Samuel. So he went from being a notorious smuggler to a man of the cloth and many of my family from then on down to my grandfather were Methodist ministers and lay preachers.

From left: Flynn Lakeman, Richard Lakeman, Leigh Genge, Andrew Lakeman

ANDREW LAKEMAN

OCEAN FISH

The Lakeman family has been resident in Mevagissey since the 1700s and has been fishing and merchanting from that time to the present day.

In the 1700s Mevagissey was founded on a beach economy with the main fishing method being beach seining for pilchards, herrings and mackerel. The only method of preserving fish was smoking (fuming), which gave fish products a life of about six months. This process was carried out in Mevagissey in three places and terminated when salt became available. Initially salting took place in 'pilchard palaces' in the village until the wet system of brining fish came on stream in the early 1800s. Many large brining tanks were built all through Mevagissey with the main tanking system being at Falmouth Cellar opposite the Congregational Chapel. The Roberts family operated from this unit with other smaller fish merchants occupying bases in other parts of the village. The Dunn family, headed by Mathias Dunn, introduced Cornish pressed pilchards to France, Spain and Italy which became the largest outlets for the product. The French and Spanish markets were soon lost but the Italians took huge quantities from Cornwall until the mid-1950s.

In the mid-1700s the inner quays of Mevagissey were constructed giving harbour protection for larger boats, which enabled the method of drift netting for pilchards in deep water. As a result of this, much squabbling took place between the seiners and the drifters, which is noted in the history books.

My grandfather, Richard Johns Lakeman, was born in 1868. He had his first lugger built at Frazier's Yard, East Quay, Mevagissey in 1904. This vessel, named Ibis, was extremely successful as it was crewed by himself and his three sons until 1930 when the new Ibis FY119 was built by Percy Mitchell of Portmellon. This new boat was 42 feet in length, 14 feet in width and 6 feet deep. My uncle Archie was the skipper, my uncle Richard the engineer and my father was in charge of the fishing gear. Once again, this boat was extremely successful and after the Second World War landed huge catches of fish. From my father's diary, on Thursday 3rd February 1949, they landed 1,291 stones of spur dogs to W Robins & Sons. On Thursday 18th May 1950 they landed 846 stones of turbot to W Robins & Sons and on Tuesday 11th November 1952, landed 2,815 stones of pilchards to Pawlyn Brothers; all record catches.

In the mid-50s many of the fishermen in Mevagissey retired and their boats were sold to other harbours. At this time the pilchard drifting was weak and in 1960 the canning factory closed. Soon afterwards all three fish merchants sold out, being J B Edwards, W Robins & Sons and Pawlyn Brothers, leaving Mevagissey empty of fish merchants. At this time the Mevagissey fishermen's co-operative was set up and ran until 1988, mainly delivering fish from Mevagissey to auction houses at Brixham and Newlyn. This business was liquidated and its assets were purchased by Edward Lakeman. Ocean Fish has been managed and expanded by him until present day.

We commenced work on West Quay and quickly moved to a new factory in Roche in 1991, where we are resident today. In order for us to enter the retail supply business we bought Riddlers of Brixham and have expanded that to become a major supplier. In the early 21st century we instigated ring netting for pilchards after going to France and learning the new method of ring netting. We now have four ring netters that were built by Buccaneer Boats Ltd, supplying fish to our freezer plants.

In 2019 we bought Stevenson & Sons at Newlyn and now operate six beam trawlers from the port, together with its fish market. For the past five years Leigh Genge has been our managing director. He is responsible for managing and expanding the business in what I believe to be extremely difficult times for the fishing industry, mainly caused by government.

From left: Edward Lakeman, Colin Langley, Lee Ells

JOHN WHATTY

"I once tried to fly. I was under five, I'd look up and see the birds flying and flipping around, they were having a lovely time. I climbed onto the roof of our house but it didn't work out quite like the birds. My knees came up and hit me in the mouth. I remember a mouth full of blood"

I am retired now but I'm still working on a boat from Brixham that was in the water for some time, hoping to get her ready by the summer. My wife Maureen managed our three angling shops, two in Meva and one in St Austell. We have our sons John and Robert – Robert we lost in an accident – and three grandchildren, James, Andrew and Megan. One of my first boats was a 30-footer *Aquarius* built by Leach and Turner in Portloe; she was lovely. I beached her near Gorran Haven and it cost me £18,500 to get her back in the water again. John Moore, the boat builder in Mevagissey did a great job. I had a good boat again.

My relations go back to the 1500s and Maureen's to the 1600s in Gorran Haven. I've come from a fishing family and always loved fishing. As a child I set fire to the house twice. It was during the war years; we had a refugee living with us who would light a fire in a boot. I thought "That was clever, I'll try that" but it kept going out. The house was lit by candle and we used paraffin for cooking back then. I got mother's five-gallon paraffin can and put the boot underneath and lit it! The next time, I thought I'd help mother by lighting the old Cornish fire, as she used to do every morning, so it was ready for cooking. She had popped round next door so I lit the fire. It kept going out, so I pushed paraffin on top of it and even the mantelpiece was on fire. I ran round to the neighbours to say the house was on fire. Well, the nearest fire station was Liskeard, the nearest phone was a mile away on top of the hill and so mother had to get a bucket down to Looe River to keep pouring water over it to dampen it down.

FRESH
FISH

BILL BEHENNA

FISHERMAN'S GRANDSON / BUSINESSMAN / KELLY'S ICE CREAM

"We have worked on the quay now for over 50 seasons!"

Bill was born in 1946, an identical twin, in a cottage in Myrtle Court, Mevagissey. His grandfather Harry was a fisherman. Interestingly, Harry was christened with an 'H' but when he grew older, the 'H' was removed. A puzzle not solved to this day.

"My grandfather, Harry and his brother George had their own boats. In fact, George's son went to Oxford University, unheard of for a fisherman's son in those days! My father was told that he should have a trade and so became a plumber here in Mevagissey. My father left Mevagissey for a brief time intending to emigrate to Canada. My mother and my brother and sisters were all ready to leave when he returned stating the weather in Canada to be too cold!

At 13, in the school holidays at Easter and in the summer, I used to work in the canning factory on the quay. We would load 1000 stone of pilchards in the factory, gut them, put them in the brine tank to sanitise them, then carry them into the part of the factory to be packed in oval tins with tomato purée. The ladies used to look after me; I never needed to take lunch. It was like working in a big family. Some nights I would go out on Jim Behenna's boat, the *Snowdrop* catching pilchards in the bay. I'd work all night and then all day. I had a lot of energy then.

At 16 I decided to join the Merchant Navy and went to Plymouth Navigation School where I became a senior cadet. At 18 I applied to shipping companies to become a midshipman. The Blue Funnel Line in Liverpool accepted me. My first trip away took me to the Far East, Australia, Tasmania and many other places. After four years I joined the Cunard company, travelling from Bangladesh and South Africa, across the Atlantic Ocean, to the USA and Mexico. A three-month trip became a ten-month trip."

Bill came home on leave and suddenly his life was to change! He had rekindled his courtship with Angela. During a storm that year the Coffee Cabin owned by Angela's father, Angelo, was devastated. Angela asked Bill if he could help him sort it out, which he did. After seven weeks, Bill was due to return to sea but Angelo begged him to stay and work for him. Initially Bill agreed to work for the summer season but was later persuaded to stay permanently. On 6th December 1969, Bill married Angela. Angelo owned a number of properties along the quay in Mevagissey, including the Coffee Cabin and the Candy Shop, now leased by the family to FatFace and She Sells.

"I went on to be a director and product manager at an ice-cream factory in St Blazey and then returned to the village to manage three businesses which included a bakery, where we baked all our own bread, pasties and cakes.

We have now worked for over 50 seasons in the village and continue to run two Kelly's ice-cream shops on the quay.

In 50 years, I've seen an amazing amount of change in the village and the fishing industry. Mevagissey fishermen have always adapted to situations, investing heavily as well, which you have to respect them for, and will carry on surviving."

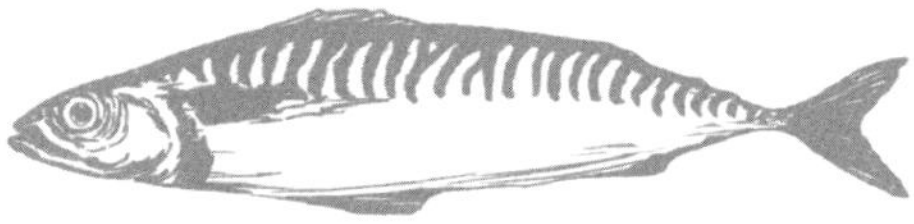

JOHN GLEESON

FISHERMAN

"The first boat I ever went out on as a child was the *Little Nell* owned by Bill Hocking at the time; I was still at school then, so I actually think that is what turned me towards the fishing. I'd just go out with him at weekends or holidays I'd go out with Bill Hocking. We'd cast trammel nets and catch all sorts"

I've been fishing most of my life. I did leave the fishing industry for a while and tried a block and bricklaying course but I just didn't get on with that at all. So I went back to sea again. I did own my own boat once and I've worked on several others' boats and can name them all and who owned them. I'm skipper on the *Vesper II* now owned by Trevor Mannell. I go off on my own fishing on that one; it has its responsibilities running someone else's boat.

I used to go out with the *Aquarius* Channel wreck netting for three-day trips at a time, twice a week and a day off. When you are out there, when it's flat and calm it's really nice to be out, it's so peaceful and no one is bothering you. You are in a world of your own. Except for when I have caught a few old war mines in the trawl! Even a bomb off Hemmick beach in my bass nets!

JOHN WILKINS

RETIRED FISHERMAN

"I'm alright Daddy, I can swim"

My first taste of fishing was with my dad and uncle. We'd go out in a small punt, angling for mackerel, from Charlestown. My first job was as an electrician's apprentice, I was paid £6 and 4d. My boiler suit cost £4 and my keep was £2, which left me with 4d to spend! I went to over to the china clay works until 1976, then went commercial fishing. I'd slowly built up gear over the years and went out by myself. I've always worked alone, working nets and pots.

I'm married to Sandra and have three grown-up children Rachael, Neil and Michaela. Very occasionally the children would go out on the boat with me. One day Rachael joined me. She had just learnt to swim and it was a glorious calm day. I was lifting the pots in a clear blue area, only about ten foot deep: you could see the ocean floor, as clear as day. Then when I started baiting and putting the pots back in the water, for a moment I forgot Rachael was there sat beside me. Next thing I knew as the pots went over, she followed them, the rope caught around her leg. She soon released herself and came back up saying, "I'm alright Daddy, I can swim."

I retired in 2021. I sold my boat but I keep my hand in by rigging nets for the local fishermen.

CLAIRE WOOD

SHIPWRIGHT'S WIFE

"Growing up in Mevagissey was the best!"

I have lived in Mevagissey my whole life and grown up alongside the younger generation of fisherman of today, many of whom remain my friends. My dad Chris Baldwin dabbled in fishing for a short while aboard Timmy Blamey's boat. I remember as a very young girl of maybe four or five, him bringing a crab home and putting it on the floor of our kitchen. I screamed and jumped up on the the worktop, petrified. However this is now a very fond memory.

It's a lovely feeling living here; you can walk along the quay and know pretty much everyone. However as a youngster this wasn't always good as everyone knew who your parents were! Being married to a shipwright you'd think would be a slightly less smelly experience than a fisherman? Oh how wrong was I! Fibreglass is a marmite smell, some love it, some hate it. I've grown to be immune to it! We have three young boys who love fishing and boats. I hope they have the same precious childhood memories that I have growing up in this amazing fishing village and community.

SIMON WOOD

SHIPWRIGHT

"I have loved fishing my whole life. I moved to Mevagissey 12 years ago where I met my now wife, a born and bred Mevagissey maid"

I started my journey here aboard a boat working out of Meva and Plymouth, and I quickly realised the intensity of the job with its unsociable hours. However the experience was like no other I have had before. I soon began to make friends with the other fishermen within the community. After this I decided to leave the fishing side and became a self-employed shipwright within the village and surrounding areas. And with an ever-growing Mevagissey fleet there is always something that needs repairing or replacing. I have received phone calls at all hours of the day and the conversation usually starts with, "Alright what's on with you?" When going to look at a job that needs doing, the allegedly "one thing" generally turns out to be a list as long as the A30.

Since becoming a shipwright I have had three sons, Ethan, Elliot and Oscar, all of whom absolutely love boats and fishing. I have no doubt that in the future they too will become involved in their generation's fishing community.

DARREN ELLIOTT

FISHERMAN

"It's a very safe feeling being amongst this fleet"

In 1970 my parents were on holiday in Mevagissey (my mum was actually pregnant with me at the time). They went out on an angling trip with John Arthur. Unfortunately, my mum was taken ill, so John had to cut the trip short to bring her back into Meva. My dad took John out for a meal to thank him and from that day, our family and John built a bond which was to start my love of fishing.

Every summer we would visit Mevagissey for our holidays and when I was older, I used to spend the whole two weeks helping John aboard his boat, the *Venus*, and then in my teens, often three or four times a year. I'd always wanted to move to Mevagissey and then in 2013, Louise and Arthur (my son, then one year old) moved here permanently. At this time, I was still working up-country as an engineer, so I would spend the time when here crewing with my fisherman friends and learning skills from them. I then did my ticket in Newlyn and in 2014, bought my own boat, the *Jackie Marie*, an 18-foot Plymouth Pilot; an old boat, but solid and sturdy. I changed my job and became a part-time fisherman.

I handline for mackerel and pollock. I've learnt the different areas to fish and the best times to be there. Although I go out mostly by myself, my son Arthur has set his sights on becoming a fisherman and jumps at the chance to accompany me on some trips. He will be one of the next generation fishermen! I've had an amazing journey. I've enjoyed learning new things and had so much support from my fellow fishermen.

ARTHUR ELLIOTT

FISHERMAN'S SON

"I went out on my first fishing trip when I was three years old"

Arthur loves everything about fishing and boats. At nine years old he has two large tool bags full of every tool you can imagine, and experiments using them on all different materials. He also creates his own Lego models of fishing boats with great attention to detail. He knows what a fishing boat should have aboard and can point out all the equipment.

"When I get older, I am going to be an engineer and go fishing as well. When I go out with Dad on the boat, I always wear my oilskins, my wellies, gloves and my lifejacket. I really like it when it is rough at sea, especially the big waves. We fish for mackerel. Dad shakes them off the line and I pick them up and put them in the boxes. Mum says if I have blood and guts all over me, she knows I've been working hard! Mackerel is my favourite fish to eat.

I go to swimming lessons every week as I know it is important to learn to swim for when I am out on the boat.

I have a punt in the garden. It's kitted out like a real boat. It has an outboard motor, ropes for mooring, two masts with lights on, a box for the fish, lots of buoys, fishing line, a life ring and weighing scales. I put on my oilskins, wellies and gloves and spend time out there in all weathers practising my fishing skills."

CHRIS BURNELL

HEAD CHEF AT THE WHEELHOUSE RESTAURANT

"No better feeling than telling customers it's come direct from the local fishermen – and it brings the heart of the village into the Wheelhouse. The quality is second to none and obviously if we were to use a wholesale supplier, it's never the same as it is straight off the boat"

We have a number of fishermen coming in of a morning after they have tended to their boats or checked their pots; they come for their coffee and talk shop between each other. Obviously sharing information on tides, fish they are catching and it's very interesting. I have learnt so much from the fishermen and they keep us up to date on the fish prices at the market and what to pay. It's a great relationship we have with them.

As a restaurant we have a licence which allows us to buy direct from the harbour. It gives us a better conversation with the customers when asked where we get our produce from. We can be guilty of taking it for granted. You have to have the licence to buy direct and register what you receive so it's within the fishermen's quota on their log books. It's beneficial as the fishing industry is able to monitor the quota, so the fish stocks regenerate themselves. It's traceability that gives us confidence where the fish comes from and passed onto the customer. It's really important that we are involved with the community and building stronger relationships with the fishermen.

ANTONIO & SUE DA SILVA

ALVORADA RESTAURANT

"I do love the fishing in Mevagissey and the people of Mevagissey are so lovely; it's a wonderful community. We stick together"

I am from a fishing village in Portugal; you grew up fishing and nothing else! I was young, I wanted to enjoy myself. I decided to do cooking and I did a five-year apprenticeship, working with top chefs, and we learnt to do everything from scratch. I came to Mevagissey 26 years ago and stayed. The people here are wonderful; good people. As long as you don't tell them what to do or change things, they accept you.

Now I catch the fish, the unusual fish that only I know how to cook, like gurnard, wrasse, spider crab, shell fish: using line or nets. I enjoy telling the customers about the fish, because I have caught it and cooked it for them. A lot of people don't always know the species of fish, or the way I cook and prepare it and present it, and the people love it. Even fish that they call 'undesirable fish' like dog or monkfish, conger eel, ling; they never knew they could be cooked with so much flavour or that they would enjoy it so much.

We fish carefully to look after our seas for the future; no one wants to over-fish, else we lose our living. I buy all my vegetables too, locally sourced, and any beef I use is from Cornwall. We have three sons who help me at times with my fishing, to get the nets in, especially the middle son; he loves to come out and help me.

The fishermen are lovely, good people too, because they talk to each other, are wise on what to catch to keep the fish stocks healthy. They are wonderful people, helping each other. The Harbour Trustees and harbour staff too; they're caring well for the harbour and fishermen; they are very united. Nowhere else can compare to Mevagissey for its community.

BOB WILSON & SPRING

"Spring and I walk on the harbour every day"

"My brother-in-law first brought me down to Mevagissey in 1981. He had a boat in the harbour called the *Aquatay*. It was a semi-commercial fishing and angling boat. I loved the place so after that I used to come down to Mevagissey often to go angling. When I married my wife, we spent part of our honeymoon here and after many holidays which followed, in 1994, we bought a house in the village and in 1995, after finishing working in London, we moved here permanently.

For the first four years I went out fishing with Tim Blamey on *Demelza* and later with Brent on the *Maria Q*. We then took on the King's Arms in May 2000 where we stayed for four years. Following that I took on the job of steward of the Social Club between 2004 and 2009."

Wherever, you see Bob, his faithful friend Spring is usually by his side, well known by the locals who meet them on the harbour on his daily walk. Bob and Geri took on Spring 13 years ago; she was then nine months old, born on Valentine's Day! She has stayed by his side through difficult times especially when Bob lost his wife to cancer five years ago.

"I've always loved music and I sell records in my online business, which Geri and I started before she passed away. I now have 21,000 records listed. I think I need to have a sort out as they are everywhere in my flat!"

JACQUELINE UZZELL

SOLOIST 'LAST POST' REMEMBRANCE DAY CEREMONY

"It is a privilege to play the Last Post as we should never forget those who gave so much for the freedom we have today"

As a resident of Mevagissey for many years and someone involved in village life, it was an honour to be asked a few years ago to play the Last Post on the solemn occasion of Remembrance Sunday at the Mevagissey War Memorial ceremony.

My father, grandfather and great-grandfather all served their country, and standing, playing the Last Post after the words, "At the going down of the sun and in the morning, we shall remember them", I am lost in the moment of silence, with no sound resonating throughout the village, whilst paying tribute to all those who served and fell.

I am also a playing member of the St Austell Band. The Band plays numerous times throughout the year in the village, as well as the Feast Week Parades, which include the Flora Dance and us leading the Carnival.

MEVAGISSEY SOCIAL CLUB

"There is a joke about Mevagissey: 'This is a drinking village, with a fishing problem.' "

The Social Club was formed in 1937 by Jack Rowe and Bill Barron, just selling beer upstairs. It became more and more popular. Before then it was the Liberal Club; they just painted over the sign and added 'Social Club'. You can go outside and just stare at the harbour in its wonder.

There is always an Albert collection tin on the bar. The Social Club gives a yearly donation of about £2000 to the Fishermen's Mission, from its weekly meat raffles. It's a fishing village and fishermen support the club and we support the fishermen. The Club has always been the hub of the harbour, especially for the fishermen.

Mevagissey was the first place to have electric street lighting too and we are proud of the fact. People are proud of their community, with its unique character. Here in the club they have a row of seats: one is called 'the fisherman's row' and the other is called 'dead man's row!' It's where the elderly sit drinking their pint and talking over old times. There are a lot of characters here still, such as 'Nick the Greek' (Nick Tomlinson) who is in his 70s and still fishing.

The Social Club will always support the Fishermen's Mission, because they know what help they give to the fishermen on a personal level. There will always be an Albert collection tin on the Social Club's bar.

Written by Chairman, Paul Wakeling

CENTRAL CAFE

CHRIS & SUE ELLIS

“We recognise the importance of supporting the Mission, having lost a good friend at sea”

Chris and Sue welcome tourists and locals alike to their takeaway chip shop and café which is situated in the village square.

‘We have been running Central Café chippy since 1991. It is a lovely village for children to grow up in. Our daughter was seven years old when we moved here and she settled quickly into the good community school.

We have always supported the Mission and even more so when Chris’s good friend Ian Thomas (Ginge) lost his life at sea in December 2011.

MEVAGISSEY WI

"Our members have fun and enjoy making new friends"

Mevagissey WI was formed in 1931 and currently has around 40 members.

It has been a very active group over the years, both within the WI and the local community. It has raised funds for the local hospices, including the Merlin Centre, and the Friends of Mevagissey Surgery. Those joining have found much fun and friendship and there have been many social and educational opportunities provided by CFWI (Cornwall Federation WI).

Members' talents in craft and cookery have been displayed over the years, in particular in the Royal Cornwall Show Competitions run by the CFWI, where there have been several winners.

Since using social media the WI has been able to reach out to a larger audience and attract younger members. The members enjoy many lunches out and go ten-pin bowling a couple of times a year. There is a craft group, a knit and natter group, a book club, a walking group, and a social activities group where gardens and various places of interest are visited. Speakers visit the monthly meeting giving interesting talks on a variety of topics, as well as some of our members undertaking workshops which include flower arrangements or displays, fused glass, stained glass, and willow craft.

The WI has a variety of activities for all ages and is always welcoming new members.

ANGELA BLAMEY

FLOWER FESTIVAL ORGANISER

"The scent of the flowers that mingles in the air is wonderful"

The Flower Festival takes place annually during Mevagissey Feast Week. It began in the early 1980s when a local lady, Marjorie Hunkin, held flower-arranging classes in the Old Bible Christian Church. A few years down the line she decided that we were good enough to hold a Flower Festival in the then church. Marjorie continued for several years and when she decided to call it a day, I took on the task. We have continued putting on a Flower Festival every year since, apart from one year, which was when we had no church as we were amalgamating with the Congregational Chapel that is now St. Andrew's. We are still continuing in the same vein: no admission charge, only donations and we always hold a quiz every year to raise money to give us a good start.

It is always a pleasure to admire the wonderful arrangements of flowers during the festival and the scent which mingles in the air is wonderful. There is always a theme each year and the displays are stunning.

JUBILEE HALL COMMITTEE

MIKE ROBERTS CHAIRMAN OF THE JUBILEE HALL COMMITTEE FORMED IN 1977

"The great difficulty is getting young people involved to help, with the physical work required in the hall, but we are proud nonetheless with what we have achieved."

The Jubilee Hall has quite some history. It was first a school and during WWII it was a school canteen and following this a community centre but it gradually got run down and prior to the Queen's Jubilee in 1977, it was decided that the hall should be completely redone and a committee was formed. Grants and funding were acquired for the roof to be replaced and to open up all the rooms to create the hall we have today. It was completed in 1978.

The committee asked me 25 years later if I would take over as chairman and obtained a lot of grants for us to rejuvenate the hall to its present function that it achieves for the community today. We must have spent at least £56,000-£60,000 at the very least, from 'Awards for All' and support from the Parish Council. The philosophy for the Jubilee Hall has always been to provide the community with a venue for the people of Mevagissey to use at the lowest affordable price, so we manage on a very small budget. Any capital projects have needed to be managed on grants.

THE ENTERTAINERS

"A pantomime again... oh yes, it is!"

Entertainment in Mevagissey began in the early 1970s with the 'Contact Club' which was held in the old Congregational Church Hall. After some years the group folded and St. Peter's Church took over. They held a pantomime every year at around Christmas time. When the church no longer organised the shows, a lady in Mevagissey called Julie Rumbles, the choreographer with St Blazey Amateur Operatic Society (AOS), took the reins and continued to direct various shows and pantomimes with village members and invited guests. She continued for many years until she became unwell and another local resident called Ann Gilder, with connection to St Austell AOS, took the lead. She produced a selection of variety shows and brought Sheila Gill in to assist. Ann taught Sheila the skills needed to create the shows.

Since then Sheila has taken on the mantle of leader and indeed, she still puts up with a raucous group of Entertainers and attempts to keep them in check. Sheila is very involved with theatrical groups in and around St Austell. With her at the helm the Entertainers have put on a range of different shows over the last few years including a play, an Old Time Music Hall and in 2019, a pantomime 'All at Sea'. The group is now rehearsing for their latest production 'Aladdin' which will be performed in the Jubilee Hall in November 2022. With familiar village characters playing Pantomime Dames and baddies it will, no doubt, be a great success. Although there is a charge for admission, all the proceeds are always shared between three local charities which are chosen each year.

MEVAGISSEY SEA SHANTY FESTIVAL

"Many voices singing as one"

If you should venture into Mevagissey in the month of October and wind your way through the narrow cobbled streets, you might be lucky enough to hear the sound of harmonies and shanties drifting on the sea air from every corner of the village and reverberating off the steep hillsides of the valley.

In 2019 the Stuns'ls, instigated the first ever Mevagissey Sea Shanty Festival, with over 30 groups, 300 singers and 11 venues. The atmosphere in Mevagissey was electric, with music spilling from every corner of the village and the promise of a rerun every year to come.

Mevagissey hosts one of the largest shanty festivals, celebrating the Cornish seafaring heritage and extending the holiday season for local businesses. The festival doesn't stop there as the profits are reinvested back into the community's different organisations and endeavours to deliver a direct benefit for all. The festival has grown over the years to a three-day event that embraces the villages of Pentewan, Polgooth, Sticker, St Ewe, Gorran Churchtown and Gorran Haven. It also fills the villages with a host of shanty crews from across the UK and Europe and boasts over 150 hours of performances between the Friday evening and Sunday lunchtime.

STUNS'LS SEA SHANTY GROUP

If there is just one thing that you need to know about the Cornish, as a race, it is that they simmer with all the emotion and wild fury of the seas, to the sounds of their coastline, and the best way to vent these emotions is to sing; and oh how they love to sing!

Stuns'ls Shanty Group just take it that one step further, blending Cornish harmonies with age-old songs of the seas and Cornish folk songs which span the centuries. The ten-strong group of singers is made up from the gig rowing veterans of Mevagissey, Charlestown and Truro, whose love for shanties and Cornish folk songs is shown in every performance. They sing every first Tuesday of the month at The Fountain Inn, Mevagissey and for the last three years have opened the Sunday music of Mevagissey Feast week.

In 2019 they had the opportunity to sing for the Duke and Duchess of Cornwall, filling the summer air with Cornish harmonies, with a backdrop of the harbour, quay and boats of Mevagissey.

BEHIND THE BOOK

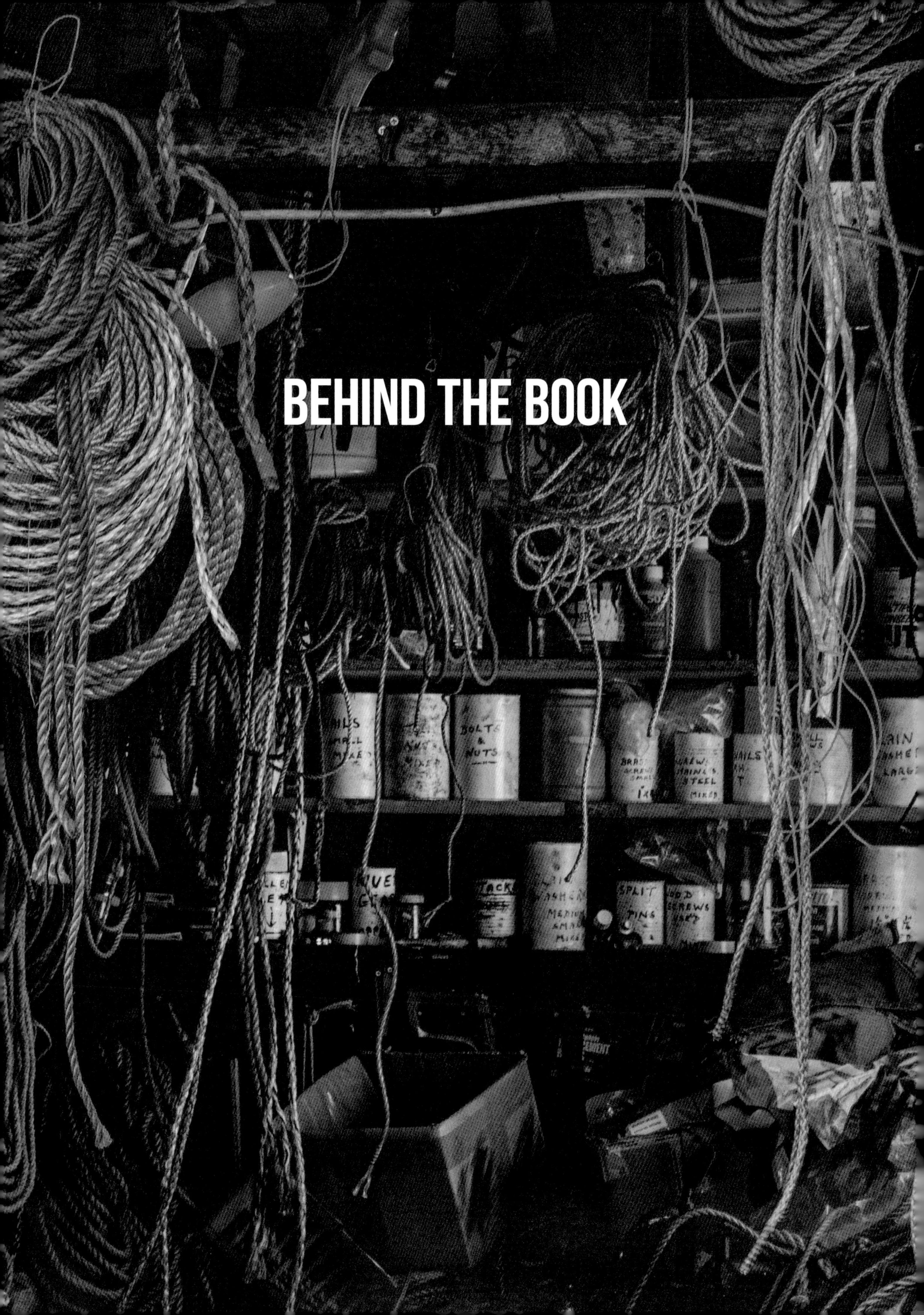

BARBARA HOCKING

VOLUNTEER INTERVIEWER

I only bought some raffle tickets off Lauren Brokenshire and the next she is telling me of her dream of creating a book about Mevagissey's fishing industry for the Fishermen's Mission Charity. All of a sudden I am sat around her table, having a cup of tea, meeting Julian Waring from the charity and creating lists of fishermen and everyone connected with harbour life.

How was I going to interview all these people that I may have never met or barely knew? But I was armed with my dictaphone and thick pink note book and I started in March 2019; a woman on a mission! I became bolder in my questions too, learning how extensive the family histories and generations are in Mevagissey and giving me fascinating insight to fishing life in all its aspects. The people are unique; honest, hard-working and courageous. They have my respect and admiration.

Nigel (my patient husband) and I both love Mevagissey since we came to live here in 2011; it's a genuine Cornish community. As a retired community midwife, it's wonderful to experience life living here with our friendships: a community with humour and attitude and beautiful surroundings and lovely people. We never want it to change.

To help me finish this book, Jill Edwards joined me with her huge smile and friendly manner, and we've truly helped and supported each other. We hope this book reveals the world of Mevagissey and its people and fishing industry, preserving the true Cornish community.

JILL EDWARDS

VOLUNTEER INTERVIEWER

I remember sitting in my lounge enjoying a cup of coffee when Barbara Hocking rang and in her gentle, encouraging voice asked me if I could help her with interviewing members of the fishing community for a book that she was putting together in aid of the Fishermen's Mission. As many of my friends know, the word "no" does not exist in my vocabulary so I jumped aboard.

At this time, I knew nothing about the Fishermen's Mission or indeed anything about fishermen other than they wore yellow wellies and owned boats in the harbour! Over the past two years how that has changed. After the initial meeting with Julian Waring, I realised how the Mission supports our fishermen and their families and recognised I wanted to help and be a part of this wonderful project. How much I have learned about our great fishing community of Mevagissey, not least the fishermen whose resilience and determination in often harsh conditions continue to bring fish to our shores. Those men in yellow wellies have incredible stories to tell and I admire each and every one of them! I've learned to recognise the different types of boats, ways of fishing and far more.

Mevagissey has a unique community and all of those who have contributed to the book make the village what it is today, one of which we can be very proud.

I would personally like to thank everyone who has helped me along this journey: particularly Barbara Hocking who gave me this opportunity and has been my rock throughout; Julian Waring for his continued support; everyone who has given their time to tell their fantastic stories; and not least my husband Alan who has put up with me tapping away on the computer keyboard for hours on end. It has been a privilege to be part of this fantastic book.

MATTHEW FACEY

PHOTOGRAPHER

I'm born and bred Mevagissey, growing up in the time of endless summers, footy against the back of the Fire Station and Zippy burgers. Much has changed but much has stayed the same. You can still find the "old" Meva if you know where to look; it's not in the shops, the posh new houses, or the empty second homes. It lives in the people and stories you read in this book, that's why it has been so important to catch this snapshot in time. It's been a great pleasure meeting the people in mine and Sally's photographs, reading the stories recorded by Barb, Jill and Julian. I hope you've enjoyed it too.

Much love to my wife, Suzy, Mum and Dad, Carol and John, and children Wills, Em and Izzy, who never fail to encourage my artistic efforts.

SALLY MITCHELL

PHOTOGRAPHER

I don't think you come out the other side of a project like this the same person as you were when you started it – you come out knowing your home town a lot better than you did before and on so many different levels.

I'm sitting trying to write something for this book on the stone bench at the end of Island Quay, the light is fading, there is the smell of salt in the wind, and I can hear the low grumble of the trawler *Ann Louise*'s engine as she moors up by Lighthouse Quay for the night. It feels like home in every sense, and I am very rooted here with family going back to the 1600s. So having the opportunity to work on a book about Mevagissey like this is an incredible experience and also carries a certain responsibility!

I worked together with Matt on the photography and I am grateful to him for his support throughout. Then, gathering all of the photographic work and interviews written by Barbara, Jill and Julian, I collated it all into this book you're holding in your hands now. I really wanted it to be a 'Meva' book, in look and feel as well as in the content and I hope I've managed to achieve that. I am indebted to Lauren Hunkin for all of her help in navigating the Meva fishing fleet – it can at times feel like a different world! This is a true team effort that I hope reflects the amazing community we have here in Mevagissey.

LAUREN HUNKIN

I've been a fundraiser for the Fishermen's Mission for many years. About three years ago Julian and I met for a coffee and I decided to get a team together to produce a book. This great team has made my vision a reality, I cannot thank these people enough for all their hard work and dedication. This book really holds some of Mevagissey's great stories and legends.

ANDREW JOHNSON

Having first become entranced by the Cornish language in the 1970s as a student, I resumed my study after retiring to St Austell with my Cornish wife and since then have started to teach Cornish both in St Austell and also online with students as far away as Spain, Australia and North Macedonia.

I became a Bard of the Cornish Gorsedh in 2020 and I am now an examiner in the language. I am delighted to be able to contribute some of the ancient but living language of Cornwall to your book and hope it achieves the success it deserves.

CREDITS

A huge thank you to Annie Butler and Mark Sweeney for their tireless proofreading work. This wouldn't be the book that it is without you both!

Pilchard Barrel original drawing created for this book by Sarah Hunkin
www.sarahhunkin.co.uk

Photo of Mevagissey Shanty Festival, page 242 – Kim Andrews

Photo of the Stuns'ls on page 243 – Helen Davies

Design and layout of the book by Sally Mitchell & Emma Gordon at www.ayr-studio.com
Mackerel drawing by Emma Gordon

Our thanks to all who supported the crowdfunding donations, some mentioned here, some anonymous. You made it possible to bring the book to print.

DEDICATIONS

From sardine tins to iron horses, in mutal solidarity, LT1143.

Phil Smith – husband, dad, grandad – always at home in Meva.

Remembering Pat Griffiths. She loved Mevagissey with all her heart.

In loving memory of Russell Over – forever fishing.

In loving memory of Mum & Dad – Norman & Valerie Blackmore.

In loving memory of Susan Macdonald who loved Mevagissey.

Karen Davis & "family", Sylvia's Emporium, The Loft, Mevagissey.

In memory of Uncle Ron & Auntie Nellie Hocking.

To Grandmother Flo Angove & my birth place. Sam Tilling.

For my mother, Diane Pearce (Nee Rowe). A Mevagissey maid.

Remembering William and Esther Chesterfield whose hearts and souls will forever remain in the village they held most dear.

For Gary & Jo Fisher, with memories of The Hoss.

Fantastic memories – Nigel & Kim Pritchard, Scott & Karl Young.

Andrew Crawshaw – much-loved Mevagissey GP for 35 years. Mary & sons.

With love from Lysanne & Stuart.

In memory of Eddie and Reenie Hutton, Norman and Lorna Facey, all lovers of Mevagissey.

FOR THE MOTHERS

Ethel Braddock, Mrs Susan James.

THOSE WHO DEDICATED A NAME

Andrews Pentewan
Kevin Atherton
Andy & Ruth Hill
Ray & Jackie Adamson
Liz Burford
Anne & Peter Middleton
Kevin Wardle
Tanith Oxley
Rupert & Penny Hayward
Roger Parramore
Pat Kelly
Sian & Steve Foster
Wendie Michie
Antonio Da Silva
Mark & Claire Heasman
Clive & Astrid Back
Alan & Sylvie Thwaites
Bob & Di Furneaux
Rob & Rachel Livingstone
Di Wells
Melanie Robinson
Will Mitchell
Hank, Heather & Jeremy Adlam
Richard & Jean Johnson
Ceila & Robin Balbernie
Fred Whittall

Doug & Joan Bishop
Mike & Annette Payne
Deborah Richards
John Hughes
Louise Fieldsend
Mike & Lindsay West
Marc & Alison Evans
Lorraine Farr
Peter & Penny Blamey
Claire Whiteley
Ben & Natalie Eglinton
Dawn Quick
Lynne & Vernon Gouldsmith
David Bates
Toni Ridgway
The Moyle family
Joshua Edward Werry
James & Sarah Jordan
Julia & Simon Goddard
Mantons of Stourport
Mark Jury
Mrs Ann Gilder
Heather Cocks
Michael Bunney
Freddie Turner
Mevagissey Sea Safaris

Elijah Bond
Isla Mei Trevarton
Clare & Tony Lea
Bill Halliday
Grant & James McKenzie
Joe Kimber
Bill Barron (Bowser)
Janet Boyle
Christopher Rowe Insurance
Jeff & Carol Eccles
Darren Camburn
Claire Vickers
Andy & Helen Smith
Davey Hal
Gayle Nykerk-Jones
Angie Barnes
Paul Wood

falfish
1142

The words in this book come from interviews and written submissions and they are not written to represent word-for-word transcripts. Rather, the author has retold them in a way that evokes the feeling and meaning what was said in all instances, the essence of the dialogue is accurate. Although the publisher has made every effort to ensure that the information in this book was correct at press time, the author and publisher do not assume and hereby disclaim any liability to any party for any loss, damage, or disruption caused by errors or omissions, whether such errors or omissions result from negligence, accident, or any other cause.

Printed and bound by Deltor Communications Ltd, Saltash, Cornwall.